The Process of God

A Practical Guide for Going from Glory to Glory

IFY OKOH

The Process of God

Copyright 2015 by Ify Okoh/Radiant Life Book House. All rights reserved. Printed in the United States of America.

No part of this book should be reproduced in any manner whatsoever without written permission except in the case of brief quotations embodied in critical articles and reviews. For more information visit: www.ifyokoh.com

Unless otherwise indicated, Scripture quotations are from the Holy Bible, New International Version, NIV. Copyright 1973, 1978, 1984 by International Bible Society. Used by permission. All rights reserved.

Scriptures marked KJV are from the King James Version of the Bible. Scriptures marked NASB are from the New American Standard Bible Copyright 1960, 1962, 1963, 1968, 1971, 1972, 1973, 1975, 1977, 1995 The Lockman Foundation. Public Domain Access.

Scriptures marked NIV11 are from the Holy Bible, New International Version, NIV. Copyright 1984, 2011 by Biblica, Inc. Used by permission. All rights reserved worldwide.

Scriptures marked NKJV are from the New King James Version. Copyright 1982 by Thomas Nelson. Used by permission. All rights reserved.

Scriptures marked NLT are from the Holy Bible, New Living Translation copyright 1996. Used by permission of Tyndale House Publishers, Inc., Wheaton, IL 60189 USA. All rights reserved.

First Edition 2015 Radiant Life Book House All rights reserved.

ISBN-13: 978-06927143 31   ISBN-10: 0692714332

DEDICATION

I would like to dedicate this book to my faithful friend, the one who knew me before I knew myself, the one who saw what I could become, who brought me out of darkness and set a table before me, the one who sticks closer than a brother—marvelous Holy Spirit. All the books in the world could not contain the expression of how awesome, beautiful and perfect you are, but if I could tell the world in one statement, it would be this: There is No Flaw in YOU!

> *Listen, for I have worthy things to say; I open my lips to speak what is right. My mouth speaks what is true, for my lips detest wickedness. All the words of my mouth are just; none of them is crooked or perverse. To the discerning all of them are right; they are faultless to those who have knowledge.*
> *love those who love me, and those who seek me find me.*
>
> —Proverbs 8:6–9,17

I am so grateful for Your Grace, Faithfulness, and Love. Heavenly Father, I am in love with you. Your love has made my life beautiful.

CONTENTS

Acknowledgments vi

Preface xi

Chapter 1   Love at First Thought. 1

Chapter 2   The Process of God 15

Chapter 3   The First Level of Glory 20

Chapter 4   Friendship Dimension 33

Chapter 5   Sons of God 41

Chapter 6   The Pinnacle of Redemption 50

Chapter 7   The Depth of Love 71

Chapter 8   God Wants Your Love 80

Chapter 9   The Most Excellent Way. 88

Chapter 10   The Counter-Balance of Grace 96

Chapter 11   The Counter-Balance of Love. 103

Chapter 12   They That Know Their God 113

Chapter 13   For Love and Glory 130

Epilogue 139

About the Author Notes 141

ACKNOWLEDGMENTS

My heartfelt thanks to . . .

My husband, Joseph. I am so grateful I get to share life's journey with you. You are my blessing, a man of steel, with a heart of gold. Thank you for making marriage easy. I love and honor you, my Eze! You are the epitome of this scripture:

Blessed is the man that walketh not in the counsel of the ungodly, nor standeth in the way of sinners, nor sitteth in the seat of the scornful. But his delight is in the law of the Lord; and in his law doth he meditate day and night. And he shall be like a tree planted by the rivers of water, that bringeth forth his fruit in his season; his leaf also shall not wither; and whatsoever he doeth shall prosper.

—Psalm 1:1–3 (KJV)

My four children: Jessica, Matthew, Frieda, and Arinze. All of you make life so much fun. Thank you for always bringing out the kid in daddy and me. You are a part of this covenant:

As for me, this is my covenant with them," says the LORD. "My Spirit, who is on you, will not depart from you, and my words that I have put in your mouth will always be on your lips, on the lips of your children and on the lips of their descendants—from this time on and forever," says the LORD.

—Isaiah 59:21 (NIV11)

My parents, Engr. Fred and Esther Nwaki, I am so blessed to be your daughter. Thank you for introducing me to the Gospel of Jesus Christ. Mom, you are truly a great woman of God; I've always wondered where your strength came from, then as I grew I found out. This scripture describes you:

She speaks with wisdom, and faithful instruction is on her tongue. She watches over the affairs of her household and does not eat the bread of idleness.
Her children arise and call her blessed; her husband also, and he praises her: "Many women do noble things, but you surpass them all." Charm is deceptive, and beauty is fleeting; but a woman who fears the LORD is to be praised.
—Proverbs 31:26–30

Dad, you are the foundation on which we all stood. Though you didn't know your dad, you are a great dad. I think you did a fine job raising six children! Thank you for your strength, your provision, your discipline, and teaching me to always stand tall, yet be willing to bend and serve. I am the woman I am because of the confidence you instilled in me. I love you, and when I think of you, this scripture comes to mind:

Train a child in the way he should go: and when he is old, he will not depart from it [I did not].
—Proverbs 22:6

A special thanks to my pastors, Bishop Dale C. Bronner and Dr. Nina Bronner of Word of Faith Family Cathedral. It is immeasurable the wisdom my family and I have applied to our lives as a result of your teachings and leadership. We are blessed to be members of this church family.

To my sisters, whom I love dearly; what would I do without the two women with whom I can laugh, cry, and scream, yet not seem diametrically opposed in nature. Thank you for being sisters indeed. To my brothers, thank you for regarding my opinions even when they were unsolicited, I love you. Thank you to all who helped encourage me when writing seemed impossible. To my mentor, Pastor Victor Oludiran, thank you so much for all your godly advice, counsel, and pushing me to step into purpose, may God richly bless you for investing in me.

Above all, thank you Jesus for all you've done—your cross. There are no words to sufficiently convey my gratitude, so:

Because your love is better than life, my lips will glorify you. I will praise you as long as I live, and in your name I will lift up my hands. —Psalm 63:3–4

PREFACE

The world is waiting for the manifestation of sons, but Jesus is returning for a bride.

Early in the fall of 2011, it was a bright and sunny day with leaves floating in the air. I was driving in my car listening to 104.7 The Fish, a local family radio station. It was a beautiful day in Atlanta, enough to lift any spirit—mine was while I drove to pick up one of my children from school. I heard the Lord say to me (a very strong heart impression), "Now study my love – for where I want you to go, you will need to know your placement in me." I knew instantly it was Him due to prior encounters, as he would go on to create the hunger for this quest I was to embark on. I had been studying wisdom and the fear of the Lord, rejoicing in the revelation of these treasures when the supernatural began manifesting in my life.

Now I thought I understood the love of God and the grandeur of the cross —"for God so loved the world that he gave his only begotten Son..." (John 3:16.KJV). But the Lord was very specific on the knowledge of the depth of this love. He wanted me to understand how to fully come alive. So I immersed myself in this quest, when I got home, I immediately pulled out my Bible and other resources to begin the journey, and for three years, it's all I have pressed-in to know.

The unveiling of the mystery of God's love is found in the key dynamics of the marriage relationship. The knowledge of God's love sets our hearts free to receive his love and live in victory, purpose, and abundance.

What is the length, breath, and depth of God's love? What does he long for us to know and experience? How do we press in for all he has made available? The truth is, he wants us to know the measure of his love, and this is how we start: He that comes to me must believe that I Am, and that I am a rewarder of them that diligently seek me (Hebrews 11:6). Diligently means steadily, earnestly, and with painstaking effort. But the reward is immeasurable. Only through a face-to-face encounter can we have the faith needed to win life's battle. **He that comes to me must believe that I Am**—that's faith, but the reward is not necessarily for the one that believes. No, it is for the seeker. What is being sought? Gold, silver, houses, riches, cars? No! The reward for seeking him is Him, and he comes with more treasure than we could ever contain. It is time for order, growth, and purpose.

In this book, you will clearly discover how to go from glory to glory. You will understand that there are levels and dimensions of Glory; how to graduate from one class to another, the rewards that come as a result of encountering God on each level. There is so much to discover, and my desire is that you press on toward that high call –to *know* him better. I unveil all that has been unveiled to me about the love of God, how much he loves us, and how to encounter this Love. I hope to guide you into intimacy with Jesus, and a hunger for a love that only comes as a result of having been in the presence of God. A revelation of God's glory and love for humanity that would help lead you into an encounter and transform your heart forever.

There is no greater adventure than to know and be known by the Creator of all things—but so few dare to dive in. We now live in a world where evil seems to be the order of the day, but the people of God must dive into God and become proxies who help stop the world from decay. This is the time for our lights to shine brighter than ever before. God has sent out his invitation. Jesus paid the price required. It's your move! Remember, the knowledge of God is not embraced with the mind, but it is marked in our hearts. God is looking for hearts that truly want to know him, and he will flood that life with light.

> We were created for him, to be one with him, and to be like him, and in that lies all the answers to the questions of life.

My prayer for you as you read this book is that your life may be transformed from the inside out, that you may come into a deeper, more intimate relationship with the Father. That you will find rest and purpose, for therein lies prosperity. May his presence abide in and on you, and cause you to ride upon the high places of life. Just as those who hosted the Ark of the Covenant prospered tremendously, may God's desire to prosper you in all things come to you as a result of his dwelling presence in your life. May you hear the voice of God within the pages of this book, and encounter purpose and revelation in the knowledge of him. Amen!

The Process of

GOD

Every Process with God is for Relationship

CHAPTER 1

Love at First Thought

"For we are God's workmanship, created in Christ Jesus to do good works, which God prepared in advance for us to do"
— Ephesians 2:10

It was love at first thought when God considered creating the human race. Man was created the moment it came into the heart of God to make him in his image and likeness. Man was first an idea before he was ever formed in Genesis 1:26, 2:7; God conceived the idea of a family before Adam came on the scene. Consider John 6:63: "The words I have spoken to you are spirit and they are life." So when God said, "let us create man", life was produced by the spirit of his words. There is a creative force in every word of God, so when he speaks, his words create. Stay with me—these are not mere semantics. Man originated from the life of God. The spirit in man, which God breathed into the vessel he formed from the dust of the ground, is the divine life of the Almighty. That life already existed in God before he put it into the vessel called man. So this idea of the human race was an actual reality in God before time began. It is why "he knew you, before he formed you"(Jeremiah 1:5). Hence, divinity remains in every human being regardless of religious affiliations or the lack thereof.

Recognizing that God loves people is the first step in helping heal the wounds of broken humanity. God loves you! Rich or poor, young or old, male or female, good or bad, and yes— ugly. He is constantly reaching out his hand to bless, to help, and to save in spite of our state. The rest of creation has been left puzzled to. The question is, why humanity? Why all the attention on this seemingly minute aspect of creation, what makes them so special and worthy of God's love, attention, and focus? Well, the answers persist in the heart of God.

Let's take it from creation, the pre-adamite world. God created the heavens and the heavenly beings, and they all served the purpose for which they were created. The moon, the sun, the stars and the galaxies in the heavens, all served his purpose and displayed his splendor. Despite the hosts of angels created to serve in the presence of pure majesty, and the splendor of the highest heavens, God was unsatisfied. There remained a space in his heart for something—a missing piece so to speak. The grand slam of all he had made was still in imagination form.

All that God created before man was for the display of his glory, but none were actual carriers of the multifaceted glory. God looked around the heavens; there was none akin to him. He wanted more. He wanted sons, ones that bore his image and likeness, united and allied. Now it would be an error to dismiss the angels who are called ministers of God. The angels of the Lord are holy, mighty, powerful, and wonderfully made. They dwell and minister in the very presence of the Most High. Nonetheless, God's idea for man would be slightly different; the concept of family was his big idea. He wanted sons, carriers of his presence and glory. God always uses natural things to illustrate spiritual things. The concept of family is one such illustration. It holds true for eternity, and demonstrates the kingdom as his household. We operate inside the kingdom through the concept of family, and we undermine that concept when we operate outside of it.

Original Intent

When God considered man, he wanted sons to be with him, feasting at his table, basking in the joy and rewards of his presence. Man would dwell with God and be co- creators, living constantly connected to the Father. Never was it in the heart of the Father to have his children apart from him. Take a look at the earth's creation process and you get a sense of God's intent. Genesis 1:3-27: God said, "let there be...and there was..." God *spoke* all things concerning the earth and the expanse of the universe into existence, but when it came to man, he made it personal. "The LORD God *formed* the man from the dust of the ground" (Genesis 2:7). Formed—molded, shaped, fashioned, designed—all of which required the use of the earth's substance. We know that a potter can only mold or sculpt holding the clay; close contact is necessary for molding. So he formed man not from a distance, but in close proximity. He touched him because he loved him, because he was his. He is a God who longs to be near, and his original intent was to have us live with him and he with us.

Jesus came to restore that place, and in his final prayer he prayed, "Father, I want those you have given me to be with me where I am, to see my glory, the glory you have given me because you loved me before the creation of the world... in order that the love you have for me may be in them and that I myself may be in them" (John 17:24-28). Man apart from God is unsatisfied and empty at best. All the money, entertainment, drugs, sex, or relationships in the world cannot fill that vacuum until he reconnects to his source—God. He deposited a Spirit in you and he longs for a relationship with that spirit (James 4:5).

We long for more because there is someone more.

War in the Heavens

Therefore rejoice, you heavens and you who dwell in them! But woe to the earth and the sea, because the devil has gone down to you! He is filled with fury, because he knows that his time is short.

—Revelation 12:12

There was rebellion in heaven. Lucifer, a guardian cherub, sinned. He was unsatisfied (putting it lightly) with God and with the position he had. He became proud on account of his beauty, though he was considered "the model of perfection" (Ezekiel 28:12), he wanted more; the problem was, he wanted the throne of the Most High (Isaiah 14:14). He just did not get the memo that Most High means **Most High**—not **most highs**, plural. It is a position for one, and God alone holds that position in the highest heaven. The Bible says wickedness was found in him; he became proud on account of the splendor God had bestowed on him. He was cast out of the third heaven where the Most High dwells, and he took with him a third of the angels under his command. He and his demons roamed planet earth. On one hand, heaven rejoiced at his expulsion. On the other, it grieved for the planet to which he fell (Revelation 12:12).

Now the earth God created was in harmony until

it encountered a force it had not known: rage, jealousy, anger, envy, slander, covetousness, pride, and all manner of evil. Satan had fallen, and throughout the earth he roamed. For the first time, the earth encountered chaos; there was discord, as one would expect from any place inhabited by wickedness, and the earth herself protested! The seas raged, the mountains trembled, the earth quaked, Satan had come to it having great wrath for what God had created. The earth is not Satan's home, he is a wanderer; he had no home until he deceived man into handing it over to him.

The Reason for Earth

The earth belongs to the Lord, but he gave man the title deed. In the midst of the land, seas, animals, birds and every living thing the Lord had created was the Garden of Eden, a place God kept for himself and man (God always keeps a remnant for himself). He carved out a territory for himself; there he visited and fellowshipped with man (Adam and Eve), away from the current untamed environment of the earth. Eden represents territory, like yeast, the kingdom of God was to spread into the rest of the earth as Adam and Eve multiplied in population and captured territories. Hence the mandate was to multiply, replenish, and subdue.

Think of it! A perfect place would not need to be

subdued or tamed; this meant something had caused what was once harmonious to rebel. God's plan was to have man take over and calm the tensions the earth was crying out against. This was to take place by establishing Eden's across the earth until harmony was restored, resources discovered and used for the expansion and rebuilding of God's domain on the earth. Keep in mind, the entire battle between the kingdom of light and the kingdom of darkness, is a battle for territory (hearts and minds). The mandate to replenish meant to make full again, build up again, and put back again—fruitful! With prudent management and the hidden treasures and resources of the earth in the hands of sons of God, the adversary would have no territory or place in which to wage war against its inhabitants.

The Reason for Man

Creation awaits sons and daughters who know their God and who they are, to become answers. We are solutions to problems, not only to fix what has been destroyed, but also to create things that have never been seen before. God has the answer to every problem that exists or that will ever exist— and that is you. We have been given a mandate as world changers: to affect how people think, live, and conduct business. We are to think big, think nations, think resources, think expansion, and think restoration. If we are going to occupy till Jesus returns, then we must control the resources of the earth.

> The creation waits in eager expectation for the sons of God to be revealed. —*Romans 8:19*

"He who has the gold makes the rules." Because the world has the gold, the world sets the agenda. But this was not meant to be—the sons of God were to have the gold. Though Adam gave it over to Satan (you are servant to whom you obey), Jesus has taken the authority from him and given it back to us. We only need to come out from our tranquilized state and begin to exercise it. The modern church is all too passive in equipping the saints for this work of ministry, not the ministry of becoming a preacher or evangelist, but the ministry to God and to humanity. We have hidden behind religious rules and traditions, and are missing out on the opportunity to change the course of history.

Religion has kept us powerless and stagnant, going around in circles, yet never making headway into the re-generated life. We are kings and priests, with the anointing for dominion when we are in partnership with our creator. Have you been given the grace for business? Go after it with fervor! Somehow we've believed the lie that if you are a Christian, you are limited in what you can do. But we are not children of a limited God. To be a successful businessperson does not make you worldly or greedy—that's religion, the feeling of guilt and condemnation. We need entrepreneurs who go after the resources for the kingdom. God gives men and women the grace for business, but many reject it because of ignorance or misguided notions. If business is your assignment and your gift to the world, do it unreservedly, knowing that you claim territory and resources for kingdom expansion as you establish kingdom principles in your area of influence.

> And hast made us unto our God kings and priests: and we shall reign on the earth." —Revelation 5:10 (KJV)

Becoming who we were born to be remains the same—multiply, be fruitful, and subdue. To multiply is to increase, reproduce, or grow. In whatever you do, successful results only come from the ability to increase in what you have been given (replication). Being fruitful, on the other hand, has to do with output—your offer to the world around you. Your assignment is to contribute to your world, make something, somewhere, or someone better. When we have dominion as believers, we take territory for the kingdom of God, and diminish the reach of the enemy.

Further Study

What new insight did you gain from reading this chapter? Read Genesis 1:1-27, 2: 28. Ephesians 2:10, Romans 8:19, Revelation 5:10, Rev 12:12

_____

_____

What were some of the attitudes of the religious people in Jesus' day?

_____

_____

What do you think your assignment is on earth, and How do you plan to accomplish it?

_____

_____

_____

Bonus Activity: A Religious Spirit is one the blinds

children of God from receiving truth. It causes us to be passive, hide behind rules and traditions, and become judgmental without the conviction to jump in and help. It is self-righteousness!

Prayerfully ask the Holy Spirit to reveal any religious spirit (mind-set) blocking you from receiving His truth into your life. Then document what he tells you, so that you can declare war against it.

Process leads to discovering who God is for you.
───────────────────────

CHAPTER 2

The Process of God

There is one glory of the sun, and another glory of the moon, and another glory of the stars: for one star differeth from another star in glory.
1 Corinthians 15:41

In the kingdom of God there are levels and dimensions of glory. It's not to suggest that one level is superior to the other, but there are different dimensions from which we can relate in the kingdom of God. We must all go through the different dimensions of truth to fully grasp what salvation is all about. Therefore; there are truths, and there are things that are more true. The kingdom of God operates by process. Everything with God is a process, and process takes you from one level of glory to another. Take a look at creation and you'll see process at work. The first process in creation required the move of the Holy Spirit. "In the beginning God created the heavens and the earth. Now the earth was formless and empty... and the Spirit of God was hovering over the waters" (Genesis1: 1-2). Likewise, any assignment God will ever send us on will require the endorsement of the Holy Spirit to guarantee a positive outcome. The Holy Spirit hovered over the waters before God said, "let there be light", process. Light had to be before creation could take place. "God separated light from the darkness... and there was evening, and there was morning— the first day" –process. "And God said, Let the earth bring forth grass, the herb yielding seed, and the fruit tree yielding fruit after his kind, whose seed is in itself, upon the earth" –process (Gen 1:11, KJV). What's the point? Understanding that process is the method for development, maturity, illumination, and excellence in every area of your life is essential in attaining anything meaningful.

We all get excited when the preacher declares, "God is changing your level" everyone gets excited, agrees with a clap, and eyes lighten up in glee. But few really know what they mean, the rest of us just want a change of level for the better, we want a change and we don't care about the details. Well, changing levels can mean different things to different people, but in the context of spirituality, and manifesting glory, changing your level means coming into a higher dimension of who you were created to be.

While God loves us all in the fullness of his love, we don't all experience him in the same measure. Whatever stage you choose to level-off in your relationship with God, is how you will experience him. You will only experience God on the level of your knowledge. For example, if you only know God as Master and yourself as servant, this is how you will experience him, and often how he will relate with you.

There are five levels in your relationship with God, and at any given season of your life one would be at work whether you realize it or not. If you are going to experience God and grow up into the full stature of Christ, you must engage in the process, press-in, and stay with it. Romans 8:19: creation is waiting eagerly for the purest, truest, most authentic manifestation of the sons of God (paraphrasing). Creation awaits the consummate man or woman to do something, be someone –be God's proxy on earth. Here are the unfolding levels of relationship in the kingdom of God. Remember, it is not that we totally graduate from each level, it's that we have been given the privilege to experience God in deeper ways.

PHASE *1*. Potter and Clay: "Like clay in the hands of the Potter, so are you in my hand" (Jeremiah 18:6)

PHASE *2*. Servant Master: "I no longer call you servants, because a servant does not know his master's business" (John 15:15)

PHASE *3*. Friendship: "I have called you friends..."(John 15:15 ASV).

PHASE 4. Father, Son: "go instead to my brothers and tell them, I am returning to my Father and your father..."(John 20:17).

PHASE 5. Lover and Beloved: " I will betroth you to me forever; I will betroth you in righteousness and justice, in love and compassion (Hosea 2:19).

The PROCESS of GOD will:

- Develop you
- Mature You
- Promote You
- Transform You
- Advance You
- Prosper You

"Beloved, I pray that thou mayest prosper in all things and be health, even as thy soul prospers" (3John 1:2).

Our souls were designed to prosper –grow; becoming more like the one from whom we came into existence. Therefore, to be born-again and not grow spiritually, will rob you of your inheritance. Imagine for a moment that your son or daughter remained in the 1st grade year after year, five years passes and they still remain in the 1st grade simply because they did not meet the requirements for advancing to the next grade level. Or, you work at a firm that keeps you at the same entry-level position for 10 years without a promotion. That would indicate something somewhere is very wrong. For our lives were designed to move forward. Anytime a persons life begins to move backward instead of forward, a set process has been violated. We live in the realm of time and we use a clock to keep a track of progression. Now if you study the clock, it does two distinct things: it keeps moving (time waits for no one), it keeps moving forward (tick, tock). So does everything in life; birth, relationships, success, sowing and reaping, creation, all happen by process. The same is true in the kingdom of God.

We have been redeemed to be Christ-like, it is our inheritance to be on an ever-increasing intensity in becoming more like the one we seek. The more intimately you know a person, the more prone you are to becoming like them. 2 Corinthians 3:18 KJV: "But we all, with open face beholding as in a glass the glory of the Lord, are changed into the same image from glory to glory, even as by the Spirit of the Lord".

God wants to take you from one level of glory into another, as your level changes in the spirit, so does blessings and spiritual gifts become more accessible to you. He wants to be known; not merely through intellectual knowledge, but by experiential knowledge. And to *know* him is to go through process _ there is no timeframe, or set order, but it is inevitable on your journey with God.

To settle for only one aspect of salvation is to rob one's

self of greater glory.

Let's begin the Process of God!

Further Study

Can you identify what Phase you are in this season of your life? If **not** Skip this question and come back after reading through to chapter.

_____

_____

_____

What are some of the significant signs/experiences that let you know you are in that phase?

_____

_____

_____

What promises have you gotten from the Lord? Jot the scriptures down.

_____

_____

_____

CHAPTER 3

The First Level of Glory

"Jesus answered and said to him, "Most assuredly, I say to you, unless one is born again, he cannot see the kingdom of God." —John 3:3 (NKJV)

The first stage in every believer's relationship with Jesus is the process of salvation. When you placed your trust in the finished work of Christ on the cross, you became a member of God's household (kingdom). You have been purchased by the sacrificial blood of Christ and are now a child of God. However, you don't know him. You may know about him, but you have simply been acquainted. In other words, he pulled you from a burning building and saved your life. Much like the first-responder firefighter, you don't know the firefighter simply because he rescued you from a burning building. But, there is certainly an elation of gratitude though you have no relationship with the person. He is your deliverer trying to heal the wounds you sustained in the fire.

Sin is much like a fire burn; it sears your heart and prevents your spirit from connecting with the spirit of God. So, it becomes difficult to have a relationship with the source from which you came. Many don't recognize the value of developing a relationship with God. We often say I have a *personal* relationship with God, but what does that relationship look like? Or, on what basis do you relate? A tangible relationship is not for the few, as some believe —the Pastor, church leader, deacon, or the super-spiritual. Jesus has been made your deliverer and your process has begun. Your salvation was the means to an end. Keep in mind that in every phase, there are four common events that will almost always occur:

1. **Promise**: God declares a promise to you. For example, he showed Joseph in a dream who he would become. (His brother's sheaves gathered around his and bowed down to it. He had yet another dream; and the sun and moon and eleven stars were bowing down to him). God declared to him his future.
2. **Barriers**: There are obstacles on everyone's journey to their promised land. It will seem like God has lied to you, what he said has no way of coming to pass from where you stand. All the hype about Christianity is not what it is cracked-up to be. Joseph was sold into slavery and it looked liked all was lost –the dreamer had been silenced.

3. **Maturity**: through whatever trails, tribulation, or pain you experience, God will be at work in you to develop your character. God will test you (not tempt you), refine you, humble you, and re-make you all at the same time. Psalm 105:19, NLT: *"until the time came to fulfill his dreams, the Lord tested Joseph's character"*.

4. **Manifestation:** all that God promised begins to come into manifestation. Because you have understood what it means to be steadfast in the midst of trails and distress to form the kind of person God can trust you with the promise.

When we think of glory, we automatically think material wealth, honor, and prominence. But the glory of God in us is what produces those things. They come as a by-product of the glory; and depending of how much glory you choose to harness, the greater your manifestation.

The glory of the new believer is that you are in; you are connected and now the recovery begins, the remolding, the breaking, and the learning. At this level, you are an heir under the custody of caregivers. Though all that the father has is yours, the resources and heritance of the house are not yet entrusted to you, because you are a *babe* in Christ. Like an infant you are learning to eat; you are being fed with milk (notice that babes are fed—they can't feed themselves). This is a critical stage because what you learn or what you hear determines if you upgrade your thinking and development. Most of what the babe in Christ knows about Jesus is often from others, such as family members, pastors, books, tapes, and occasionally a verse or two of the bible. The Bible is not a book that necessarily charms a *babe*; not because it is of no importance but because a relationship has not yet been developed. The knowledge of the Holy Spirit is also foreign, as the new believer is not able to relate with the idea of his indwelling, though he has heard it preached.

Nevertheless, you belong to Christ and he has begun his work in you, reshaping and remolding, often without your awareness. You may find that you want to know this Jesus who saved you by attending church services, though you are not necessarily involved with the things of the kingdom either personally or publicly. You'll make mistakes, babes do—it's actually a good thing as you are learning how your new man responds to the old. When the sculptor is handling the clay, it is uncomfortable—things fall off and things are put back together. All this is evidence of a transformative work being done in your life. At this level, the potter does most of the work, if not all the work; and your response to the process would determine how fast you progress to your next phase.

The Master-Servant Dimension

> Now I say, That the heir, as long as he is a child, differeth nothing from a servant, though he be lord of all.
>
> —Galatians 4:1 (KJV)

Your life can only change commensurate to the knowledge and the application of it to your life. Going from one glory to another will require a different way of thinking. If you think like a servant, you cannot walk like a king. It is imperative that we grow in knowledge, and also apply it once we have it. The second phase in the process of changing our spiritual level, is the master-servant dimension. The *Master-Servant* dimension is slightly different from that of the *Potter-Clay*; the servant is in— and an active member of the household. For the sake of this illustration, the word servant here does not mean pastor, minister, leader, man or woman of God in any sphere of society. This servant is a servant in the realm of the spirit because of their knowledge of the Father. Let's go a bit deeper. " It is the glory of God to conceal a matter, and the honor of kings to search them out" (Proverbs 25:2, KJV). This verse is giving us a spiritual picture of how the heavens see those who are working with revelation knowledge. But as you know, hardly is a servant given the privilege of eating at his master's table. Although you have been given the keys to the kingdom, you may not have access to what belongs to you (your inheritance).

We are of the household of God according to Paul the Apostle, in Ephesians 2:19. And in 2Timothy 2:20, he talks about the differences of value in that great house. "Now in a large house there are not only gold and silver vessels, but also vessels of wood and of earthenware…" This gives us the picture that although we are all members of Gods family of believers, not all are at their fullest potential in the house. It therefore becomes imperative that we not only become aware of that fact, but also begin to engage in the necessary requirements to move higher. God expects this of every believer. He has not called us to a life of insignificance but to one that cannot be ignored. "You are the light of the world. A city set on a hill cannot be hidden" (Matthew 5:14, ESV).

One of the main reasons we must out grow this posture is, masters are obligated to care for their servants, but the servant is not free in his master's house nor is the master free to disclose personal information. The servant lacks insight, and most of what the servant sees are chores —the do's and don'ts. It goes something like this, God can't you see what I'm doing for you? I don't steal, curse, or drink; I don't commit adultery, why are you blessing so and so, but not me —what am I doing wrong? The problem is not what you are doing or not doing right, but rather, the position of your heart.

Servant hardly fully delight in their masters, and so they must put up appearances; much like the religious they have an outward appearance of godliness, but lack transformation. So you can know God, but have not been transformed because of your level of intimacy.

If you are not experiencing transformation – becoming a new creature that is; if you don't know what God is doing in your life, have never received a promise *directly* from God, chances are, your relationship with God is that of *Master-Servant*.

Let's come a little closer. Remember the story of the prodigal son? Not the one who left, but the older one who stayed. Luke 15:28 (NIV): "The older brother became angry and refused to go in. So his father went out and pleaded with him. But he answered his father, 'Look! All these years I've been slaving for you and never disobeyed your orders. Yet you never gave me even a young goat so I could celebrate with my friends". At close look, the older son helps us understand his level, though he had access to the glory of his father's house, he saw himself as a servant, he called himself a slave. "All these years I've been slaving". He was self-righteous, "I never disobeyed your orders;" he wanted to earn his fathers inheritance. But as we know, the whole point of an inheritance is that it cannot be earned, you must simply be positioned for it.

Just because you serve in church, sing in the

choir, or even preach from the bible, does not mean that you *know* God intimately. As a matter of fact, too many today speak for the God they hardly *know*. Contrary to popular teaching, knowing God is not automatic; you may know about him, you could be sound in your ability to quote and divide scripture, but until have an encounter with the author of the word, all you have are the letters of the written word –Religion! The Pharisee knew the law but had no relationship with the law-giver.

An intention to move closer in intimacy must be developed in other to change your spiritual level. When you begin changing in the spirit (transformation), your mind, soul, and body begin manifesting what has been deposited inwardly. Until our minds are renewed, there cannot be a change of levels. Philippians 2:12 "work out your own salvation", meaning you must do what is necessary to manifest what has already been deposited in you.

Way too many of God's children stay in this level for longer than is necessary, relishing in the fact that they are God's servant, they think intimacy with God is for the few that preach/ teach them. It is partly why we have too many with un-renewed minds in the body of Christ, tossed back and forth by every wind of doctrine (Ephesians 4:14). Why? Servants are infants, and infant are not entrusted with secret things, nor are they entrusted with the heart of their master. So don't settle for a mundane Christian life, fight for all the possibilities salvation makes available. Your destiny is an adventure not a destination, so if your journey with God does not seem like an adventure but a chore, it is time to move to another level.

1Corinthians 15:41: *there is the glory of the star, and one star exceeds another in glory* (paraphrasing). So it is in measure that glory is manifested

Don't misunderstand, we all must serve at every level, the kingdom is about serving in whatever sphere you find yourself. The only difference between the services is the depth from which it is comes. For the purpose of this teaching, we are making servitude not the ultimate position of attainment.

Naturally, the master gives orders, and the servant carries them out. There is no intimacy, no insight, just commands. The servant cannot have revelation or insight into the heart of his master or the plans for his house because, "a servant does not know his master's business" (John 15:15). There is no intimacy. It is often why we find people who serve in the church, but do not reflect the God they serve.

A common trait of the servant mentality is: they possess a beggarly attitude. They are often begging God to bless them—not that it's wrong to ask God for blessings, no, but they beg because they lack confidence in the willingness of One who can answer; assuming the Master does not want to give it freely. There is no established trust between the two. Remember the prayer of Jesus at Lazarus' grave, (John 11.41-42) "Father, I thank you that you have heard Me. "I know that you always hear me;" That is a place of complete trust but two people who truly *know* themselves. Now do you see why you can't stay at this level?

On this level, the servant is on milk—okay, maybe with a little cereal! If we are not careful, we could develop a heart motivated by tasks, trying to earn the approval of the one we serve, and religion is often glad to step-in and pacify the unsatisfied. But, proximity is the servant's advantage; exposure to the master's acts (miracles, testimonies, prophesy, healing, provision, etc.) gives room for imminent growth; as observation can be a good motivator. Or frustration on the other hand, can be the catalyst that provokes a need for change. When this happens, there is an opportunity to step into knowledge.

And I, brethren, could not speak unto you as unto spiritual, but as unto carnal, even as unto babes in Christ. I have fed you with milk, and not with meat.
—1 Corinthians 3:1-2

If you're only with your Bible when it's time for a Sunday service, feel pressured to walk out the Christian life, or not sure of God's love for you besides what has been told you, you need an upgrade. You see, as a believer, your thirst has been quenched, but if you don't have hunger, you have not "tasted" and "seen" yet. The hunger never goes away!

Many tend to stay at this stage for a long time, it is often the greatest transition point for the believer, [Religion vs Relationship] form vs. transformation. Remember, we all determine how long our process will take. **The** Law of Process written by John c Maxwell says "As long as a person doesn't know what he doesn't know, he isn't going to grow". **(The 21 Irrefutable Laws of Leadership, 10th Edition, pg.27).** God does not measure time he measures growth –it's your move!

<u>Further Study</u>

Requirement: You need a place where you will be taught kingdom realities and principles to help expand your capacity. A victorious life demands the enlargement of your capacity to handle truth. Your capacity to develop will distinguish you in the realm of the spirit.

How did you come to Christ? Record it!

_____

_____

_____

What is your relationship goal for intimacy with Jesus and his Holy Spirit:

_____

_____

_____

_____

Self-study will help speed your process up. Jot down your plan of study?

_____

_____

_____

Why did you accept Christ as Lord? (Remember, this exercise is for you to realize your intention for loving Christ at this stage). See how it changes as you progress!

_____

_____

_____

_____

_____

Process will Upgrade You.

CHAPTER 4

Friendship Dimension

I no longer call you servants,... Instead, I have called you friends, for everything that I learned from my Father I have made known to you. **– John 15:15**

Friendship is the attachment of one person to another by affection or esteem. Unlike a servant, a friend is motivated by the qualities of a relationship: communication and acceptance. God likes friends, and he goes to great lengths for his friends. Just ask Abraham, Moses, and David. They all had three things common to friends of God: intimacy, a covenant promise, and purpose. There are many other benefits, but if you have not received these three, you will need to press in to the secret place until you receive from him these guaranteed rewards that are a natural response for having been with the King. Always remember, he is the reward.

Hebrews 11:6 says, "He that cometh to God must believe that he is, and that he is a rewarder of them that diligently seek him" (KJV). Let's take this verse apart for a better understanding. First, "he that cometh to God," that's you, believing that "he is" is a belief based on faith of who he says he is. At the servant dimension, he has shown himself and the possibilities to be experienced with him, and you are convinced he is as he has said.

Now the big reward! Wait for it...it's him! He rewards you with himself, his manifested presence, which is far greater than anything we may ever want or conceive in our limited thinking. He gives us himself, and that's what Proverbs 8:19 says: *My fruit is better than fine gold, what I yield surpasses choice silver*. Jesus is the greatest reward we can ever receive. When he becomes your friend, he makes available the necessities in life. In his presence is life, peace, joy, faith, promises, purpose, revelation, insight, and foresight—just to name a few. Don't try to go for the gold first; go for the one who is the priceless treasure and the gold will be yours as well_ he beautifies wherever he lives.

Knowing God as friend comes as you desire or delight in your relationship with him. The more you delight, the more He shows up and introduces himself in new ways. How do you get access into this position? Revelation! Revelation upgrades your status in the realm of the spirit.

In the friendship stage, God gives access by way of revelation to who he is and also who you are. Your knowledge of him grows considerably, and you are in the house for some quality time. As a friend, you are privy to some of the things he has available – kingdom realities. He will only let you in however, on what you can handle. Friends can only handle so much of who you truly are. So it must grow and develop. The test of friendship is trust. There will always be tests you'll have to pass; only this time, you may be aware that you are taking a test. Your spiritual radar is shaper, and he'll let you know how you are doing—as good friends often do.

When you develop communication with God, you gain more confidence in him as you better understand his Word, character, and nature. As you make it your routine to spend time with him, this instruction will serve you well: "Son of man, let all my words sink deep into your own heart first. Listen to them carefully for yourself" (Ezekiel 3:10 NLT). God is saying come in, sit down, and stay a while. This is an intentional step toward growth.

Here you get acquainted with the Holy Spirit, though you may not altogether relate to the Holy Spirit as you do the Father. With this new level, your friend would often serve you lunch; show you wondrous things out of his Word. When God pours his love on you, gives you instruction, revelation, or insight, you are feasting at his table. When you are a friend, you can better understand his likes and dislikes. The servant does not understand, doesn't even think they are supposed to. When God becomes your friend, he can confide in you. You share a fellowship, as you tell him what you think of him, and he tells you what he thinks of you.

Requirement: You'll have to want to be a friend. Graciously he initiates the friendship, but he backs off to see if you are willing to explore a deeper relationship with him also. He wants to be pursued, much like a woman longs to be. He wants you, but no doubt, he wants you to want him (Jeremiah 29:13–14). He will not give his friendship to an unwilling participant. Abraham was called a friend of God. Why? He found God worthy of chasing after.

    The Bible says Abraham obeyed God and it was accounted unto him for righteousness. Friend of God—what an amazing title! An earthling in friendship with divinity. This is one of the stunning concepts of God_ relationship. As previous levels indicate, it is possible to be a child of God and not a friend. Though we might develop our relationships in different ways and at different paces, Our process will always be ongoing, it is the result of learning, persistence, perseverance, and self-discipline. Abraham was willing to go to any length, including sacrificing his son, to prove his love and loyalty. The truth is, a genuine friendship would always include making sacrifices, otherwise that is a superficial friendship. "A man that has friends must show himself friendly: and there is a friend that sticks closer than a brother" (Proverbs 18:24 AKJV). The latter is the Holy Spirit!

Much as you need a plan for personal growth and development, you need a plan to grow spiritually. Peter puts it this way " grow in grace and in the knowledge of our Lord." Friendship is an amazing experience, but if you stay at any one level for too long, eventually it loses its wonder. Don't level off when there are opportunities to grow and expand. Exodus 33:11 (AKJV) says "the LORD spoke to Moses face to face, as a man speaks to his friend" (AKJV) If you have cultivated a friendship, your growth will soon begin to show.

Further Study:

Seek the face of God for relationship not needs. Take Note of what begins to happen that you cannot explain in your natural mind

_____

_____

_____

_____

God will test you (free notice) on anything he wants to become a part of your life. For instance, if he tells you to be courageous, there will be situations where you will have to exercise courage. There is no pass or fail, just development, until it becomes a part of who you become.

_____

_____

_____

Record any area in which you think God maybe testing you (Patience, fear, peace, kindness, courage, discipline, faithfulness, etc.). NOTE: God will never test you with any sickness or disease.

The main requirement for changing your level is that you grow in the Word. Carve out a personal bible study time and record any scripture that comes alive to you.

Invite the Holy Spirit to take you deeper. Ask Him for him and nothing else!

Like newborn babies, crave pure spiritual milk, so that by it you may grow up in your salvation, now that you have tasted that the Lord is good." —Peter 2:1–3.

Process Leads to Your Inheritance.

CHAPTER 5

Sons of God

For as many as are led by the Spirit of God, they are the sons of God _ **Romans** - 8:14 (KJV)

Every believer is a child of God, but not every believer is a son. The word son here refers to *huios* in Greek, which means *mature*. If you stopped at this level for the rest of your life, you would have made a great advancement in the kingdom and on earth (they work hand in hand). The father-son relationship is what Jesus came to reveal, and that bond is quite transformational. It is a position of privilege and authority, blessing and inheritance. The transcendence of sonship is certainly one that surpasses that of any friendship. While friends do care for one another and are attached by affection or esteem, the concept is still fragile in comparison. To be a son has to do with kinship, and at redemption there are five different realms of development parallel to that of our physical growth. Each of these dimensional stages reflect our positioning on a spiritual levels that have been outlined above. The Greek rendering helps our understanding of this process, as the New Testament is where we find the call to push into higher realms in God.

Stage 1. We begin at nepios.[1] With salvation, a translation into the kingdom of God occurred. Although a son, the nepios is a spiritual babe or an infant just born into the kingdom. Much like the clay, babes are yet unaware, unskilled, and untaught.

Now I say, That the heir, as long as he is a child, differeth nothing from a servant, though he be lord of all; But is under tutors and governors until the time appointed of the father. Even so we, when we were children, were in bondage under the elements of the world: But when the fullness of the time was come, God sent forth his Son, made of a woman, made under the law, To redeem them that were under the law, that we might receive the adoption of sons. And because ye are sons, God hath sent forth the Spirit of his Son into your hearts, crying, Abba, Father. Wherefore thou art no more a servant, but a son; and if a son, then an heir of God through Christ.—Galatians 4:1–7 (KJV)

Stage 2. Paidion:[2] spiritual adolescent; still

immature but growing. The paidion, like the servant, is getting to know the master but still struggles with the fallen nature as it relates to understanding, knowledge, and godly living. But he familiarizes himself with the master of the house, developing habits from the house; thereby growth in relationship can be rapid.

Now in a large house there are not only gold and silver vessels, but also vessels of wood and of earthenware, and some to honor and some to dishonor. Therefore, if anyone cleanses himself from these things, he will be a vessel for honor, sanctified, useful to the Master, prepared for every good work. Now flee from youthful lusts and pursue righteousness, faith, love and peace, with those who call on the Lord from a pure heart.—2 Timothy 2:20–22 (NASB)

Stage 3. Teknon:[3] is young adulthood; John uses this term in 1 John 2:13 in relation to young men who have overcome the old nature. The teknon believer is now a devoted follower of Christ and is learning from the teacher. The teknon is a friend getting insights from his friend and conforming to his friend's principles and ideals. With regular fellowship at this stage, you should be hungry for more.

But what things were gain to me, these I have counted loss for Christ. Yet indeed I also count all things loss for the excellence of the knowledge of Christ Jesus my Lord, for whom I have suffered the loss of all things, and count them as rubbish, that I may gain Christ...that I may know Him and the power of His resurrection, and the fellowship of His sufferings, being conformed to His death.—Philippians 3:7–8, 10 (NKJV)

Stage 4. Huios:[4] the mature in Christ, is Spirit filled and Spirit led. Totally committed to the Father and possessing the fruits of the Spirit. This is the sold-out stage, which comes with many sacrifices for what he wants, rather than what we want. You are intimately walking with the Holy Spirit and have chosen Jesus above all else (people, possession, reputation, and selfish-ambitions) that doesn't line up with his agenda. This is the stage of manifestation; the huios is fully trained, skilled and equipped; the world is waiting to hear you. You can stop here as many do, and this would be sufficient enough for fruit bearing and carrying out every good work. But—there's more! Hallelujah.

I have been crucified with Christ; it is no longer I who live, but Christ lives in me; and the life which I now live in the flesh I live by faith in the Son of God, who loved me and gave Himself for me. —Galatians 2:20 (NKJV)

Stage 5. Telios:[5] This is the realm of greater glory and it is often achieved by the committed minority. This is a son in complete unity with the Father. This stage is not required and only voluntary; it is a place where you act and think like Jesus. You are God's proxy and you know it! When you walk into a room, it becomes as though God walked in. The signs and wonders dwell in this realm, having the ability to affect an atmosphere. A realm of oneness—Jesus prayed that we would be one just as he and the Father were one (John 17:21–23)—that we would come to a singleness of purpose with God. The teilos has gotten to his end and is no longer striving with God; there is no self-involvement; he has totally abandoned self to love and serve Christ. The telios is the consummate man or woman of God. And this is the bride Christ wants to return for.

"But if the servant declares, 'I love my master and my wife and children and do not want to go free,' then his master must take him before the judges. He shall take him to the door or the doorpost and pierce his ear with an awl. Then he will be his servant for life."— Exodus 21:5–6)

Sonship Dimension

At this level you are considered a son, the **huios** of God—both male and female are considered "sons" in the kingdom of God. A mature son by God's definition is one who is fully trained. A significant relationship with the Holy Spirit has been cultivated and he is real to you. The source of strength for the son comes from quiet times in prayer, worship, Bible study, and meditation. It's God's gift of hunger for his sons, Jesus said in Matthew 5:6: "Blessed are those who hunger and thirst for righteousness, for they will be filled." The thirst is quenched, but the hunger never goes away once you have tasted of his presence. The call is for more and more!

God speaks to his sons through various means, such as dreams, visions, impressions of the heart, but primarily through his Word. He lets you in on secrets and mysteries, and you desire to be more like Jesus—as a son to his father. Now the Father trusts you enough for service as it relates to what he wants done on the earth. Keep in mind that all creation at this point is groaning for the manifestation of who God has called you to be.

The son walks securely because the father guarantees his protection; he is free from the fear of man and demons. Some other benefits to being a son are revelation and insight into the deep things of God; the Holy Spirit unveils the Scriptures and the mind of God concerning an issue, frequent updates (infilling), and intimacy.

Sonship requires sanctification, sacrifice, and service—you are set apart for the Father's purpose. The son of God must pursue holiness "...without which no one will see the Lord" (Hebrews 12:14). Access is granted to the face of God on the earth; that is, we can see him through the eyes of our hearts as we gaze on Lord. It is the reason you can truly say I know him, because our heart sees him. You have knowledge by experience, you have Epignosis –Exact knowledge.

"Blessed are the pure in heart, for they shall see God" (Matthew 5:8 NASB). This is not for when we go to heaven but here on earth. A pure heart is a heart that increasingly wants to know him.

The Holy Spirit is always working on our hearts, drawing us deeper into God. And this hunger never ceases unless we stop the process. Worship is critical to our development, as it is often the quickest way to connect with the Spirit of God. Worship is not just in the singing or the instruments, though they help set the atmosphere. Worship is a matter of the heart.

How lovely is your dwelling place, O LORD Almighty! My soul yearns, even faints, for the courts of the LORD; my heart and my flesh cry out for the living God

—Psalm 84:1–2.

If you find that there's got to be more, there is! Jesus came to reveal the Father, that was the glory he came to display. But he himself said: " I have many things to tell you, but you cannot bear them now, but when he, the Spirit of Truth comes, he will guide you into all truth."(John 16:12)

All truth, not some truth—ALL Truth. The Holy Spirit has come to reveal the greater glory destined for you. He saved the best for last, and that is the pinnacle of redemption.

Further Study

Requirement: This level in your spiritual life will require commitment and delightful obedience.

_____

_____

It will also require that you break through difficulties and face challenges that many are not willing to pay the price for.

_____

This level is sustained through unwavering commitment. Still want to go further?

_____

_____

_____

_____

Process Manifests Fullness

CHAPTER 6

The Pinnacle of Redemption

"Every man at the beginning doth set forth good wine; and when men have well drunk, then that which is worse: but thou hast kept the good wine until now." - John 2:10 KJV

As you recall in our previous chapters that scripture uses different metaphors to describe our relationship with God. Each depiction brilliantly speaks of the various aspects of our spiritual growth and the various aspects of God's heart towards us at different seasons of our lives. Notice that it ascends in an astonishing way, to display different levels in intimacy. It grows more radiant and stunningly rich as we discover the pinnacle of redemption.

Ever wonder about the significance of Jesus turning water-to- wine? Couldn't he have chosen to perform any number of miracles, heal the sick, cast out a demon or two, or respond to faith? The answer as you know is yes. Yet, he chose to turn water to wine at a wedding ceremony by no coincidence. Much revelation lies in this miracle and its significance to the body of Christ. Read on, and you'll love it.   First, let's dismantle the argument that the water Jesus transformed into wine was without alcohol –not encouraging alcohol, but the Greek translation is oinos, meaning "fermented wine," or fermented grape. When grapes have been through fermentation, the conversion of sugar into alcohol and carbon dioxide, the result is grape juice with alcohol, known as wine. This is important because it helps us better understand the unveiling of this mystery.

So Jesus was invited to a wedding in Cana of Galilee when the wine at the ceremony ran out. By Jewish tradition of the day, it was not reputable to run out of wine during a feast. Ok, It was outright irresponsible. Well, Jesus saved the day at his mother's intersession and the water was turned to wine. The Bible say's by this miracle "he revealed his glory" (John 2:11). Jesus first revealed his glory at a wedding—not primarily to display his divine abilities, for his disciples to put their trust in him, nor was it to prove he could make better tasting wine. He did this for the main purpose of displaying a stunning mystery— that is, God as Lover (Bridegroom) and we his bride.

Now, you will need to put off any religious cloak if you would grasp the most intimate metaphor God uses to describe the kind of relationship he is inviting us into. If you will open your heart to the idea that Jesus didn't come only to set you free from sin, make you his disciple, and give you the title "Christian", you'll find that the pinnacle of redemption is a call to the greatest love story ever told.

"As a bridegroom rejoices over his bride, so will your God rejoice over you" (Isaiah 62:5).

True life in the kingdom of God is a celebration, regardless of what is happening to or around you. God is rejoicing over you He's got you, and he believes he's got a great prize. If you can believe this, it will transform you forever. It's the reason Jesus endured the cross. To bring us into a realm of intimate fellowship with God and that is what spirituality is all about. It is not in the multitude of our religious activities, or in the excellence of our executions, or in our disciplines. No, to be spiritual is to be in intimacy with God, and from that place we can operate in righteousness.

Back to the miracle! True transformation comes through the infilling of the Holy Spirit. Jesus first needed to fill six pots (six, the number of man) with water (the Word). Only when we are filled with the living Word (baptism of the Holy Spirit), can we fully be transformed. If we shrink back from this level of intimacy, we settle for measure instead of the fullness of our glorious inheritance. The Holy Spirit is the wine, when a person experiences Him, it's intoxicating, hence the importance of the wine.

The Story of Marriage

The story of marriage is the story of redemption. It is where heaven meets earth to give us a life blooming with possibilities. The best paradigm in the bible that illustrates the relationship God want to have with us is that of the bridegroom and his bride. It is why the first miracle of Jesus is the most significant mystery for these last days.

In the dynamics of marriage, life changes dramatically, while a son can inherit his father's blessings and possessions, a wife's true inheritance is her husband. Stay with! It is a total shift. Though our modern day culture might make this a bit difficult to accept, but in marriage, everything the man has becomes the woman's, and everything the woman has becomes the man's. They become **one (inseparable)**. Jesus surrendered his life to give us an eternal one, we in-turn surrender ours that we might gain his. Though it seems to good to be true, it is a kingdom reality! God is the hero in his great story and like any extravagant Lover, his bride is the victim of all his goodness_ and that's a pretty good place to be. All that Jesus has been given is ours, sequentially, all our baggage (fears, insecurities, sicknesses, diseases, poverty, etc.) he gets to take because he paid the price for them.

Being the beloved of God requires an adjustment in the way we see ourselves. It requires stepping into your truest identity. The way we see and experience him will help determine if we enter into the fullness of our inheritance. We cannot enter into our fullest destiny with God unless we allow ourselves receive all that salvation bought. He is our inheritance, and he is waiting for us to claim it!

Salvation was God's means to an end —that he might have you. God's ultimate plan was for fellowship. A partnership which involves two walking together in agreement. It is not to say everything become a breeze, far from it, ask anyone who's been married for some time. They'll tell you becoming one is a process of learning, some distress, surrender, sacrifice, and pure joy. The process of God is no different. It is in the process we grow more like him. We are not to approach it as an obligation to fulfill, but an alluring invitation to abide.

It's a place of changing water to wine, an experience with the Spirit of God that leads us to take hold of him and not let go. It's a place of ownership, where you by experience are the one whom Jesus loves. You no longer know it merely in your head but in your heart.

"Listen, listen to me, and eat what is good, and your soul will delight in the richest of fare" _Isaiah 55:2.

Because God always saves the best for last, we are invited to a banquet filled with wine. Just as Wine intoxicates, experiencing God as Lover is the highest point of development. It doesn't get any better than that. When you have tasted of your lovers wine, "the sweetest of loves", you discover his fierce devotion to you. This Lover never divorces his bride, it is eternal, and there is no fear in this kind of love. Only through the most intimate of relationships can you *know* the beauty of the One who knows you most and loves you passionately.

God wants to bring you into this life, a life that knows him as the lover of your soul. To experience scriptures like, "I am my lover's and my lover is mine" (Songs 6:3), "I will betroth you to me forever" (Hosea 2:19). " I have loved you with an everlasting love" (Jeremiah 31:3). "for your husband is your maker" (Isaiah 54:5). The truth is that our hearts are desperate for the true freedom of his love. A love that washes away past, present, and future sins. You have been washed and presented to God holy and blameless. Walk it out!

Christ loved the church and gave himself up for her to make her holy, cleansing her by the washing with water through the word, and to present her to himself as a radiant church, without stain or wrinkle or any other blemish, but holy and blameless (Ephesians 5: 25-27).

We cannot afford to be satisfied with just having the title, Christian or Pastor, Christ ought to be found in us, and we in him. We are to become like him. It's the whole point of the process, and these dimensions in relationship give us a roadmap into the transition. During the first few years of a marriage, a woman is the still the product of her parents and her upbringing, after she has been married a while; she is the product of her husband whether positively or negatively. If you have been with Jesus a while, he ought to be seen in the way you conduct your life. The story of the rich young ruler is a good example of what happens when we lack relationship.

The bible lets us know that he was very familiar with the word, but he did not have a relationship with the living Word (Jesus). "All these I have kept since I was a boy," (Luke 18:21) he said. He kept the law, but having the word and keeping it without a relationship or fellowship, will give you religion every time. He was invited into a relationship, but as we understand, he went away sorrowful. Sorrowful! When he was being offered everlasting joy.

Don't pass up relationship for routine, remember the story Mary and Martha. "Martha, Martha," the Lord answered, "you are worried and upset about many things, but only one thing is needed. Mary has chosen what is better, and it will not be taken away from her."_ Luke 10:38- 42

Hopefully, you've read the story of Martha and Mary. Martha was busy preparing a meal, a complicated meal, obviously, because she was overwhelmed. Only one thing was needful, and no, it wasn't a less complicated meal. Jesus went straight for the issue. It was a matter of the heart. Jesus captivated Mary; all she wanted was to be close to him, to learn from him, Love personified! She recognized who Jesus was, and left everything to sit at his feet and turn her heart toward his majesty. Our hearts were made for worship. Mary worshipped by letting all go just to be with Jesus. And the gift of presence was **not** going to be taken away from her.

The first time we see the move of the Holy Spirit in the book of Acts, the onlookers thought the people were drunk. The Presence can also overwhelm us like wine. You see, Water does not alter the state of the drinker's character, attitude, or behavior, but wine does. Water quenches thirst, but wine intoxicates. What if this is why many go to church weekly, receive the word, but are not fully transformed. We cannot rely simply on water, we need the wine, the Spirit, the Presence that sets our hearts ablaze and our eyes on fire. Nothing else will do if we are to carry out exploits for the kingdom of God. Where we operate by a superior authority, become unafraid. We must take the stronger drink and come into maturity. To buttress the wine metaphor, a consistent drink of the wine is needed to remain intoxicated. No matter how good a drunkard one is, yesterday's wine won't keep you drunk tomorrow. A regular intake is necessary for effect. And you become addicted to the best addiction a person can have.

Intimacy

"You are of the household of God" Ephesians 2:19 (NKJV)

Just like in a house, the closest relationship is that of the husband and the wife, the closest dimension in relationship with God is when we become aware of our bridal status in him. Not many realize that they can experience God as Lover, no wonder the world finds it difficult to see our beauty. The beauty of a woman radiates when she knows she is greatly loved. Cut off from it, she is rather plain, uninviting, or lacking radiance. Though her beauty still lies within, it is restrained and suppressed. God longs to love us the way he ordained a husband to love his wife, not " Jesus loves me, this I know, for the bible tells me so". No, He wants to bring us unto himself and love us in full measure. A love so captivating, so astonishing, it lights our hearts ablaze.

God has saved the best for last, as in any great love story, the hero gets the beauty, a mature bride who actually knows him. This is a dimension of utter glory and splendor, knowing that he is ours and we are his. We the bride and he our Bridegroom (Lover and Beloved). Marriage is a place of rest, beauty, peace, joy, and celebration. It is a place of intimacy and close union. A place of confidence, security, trust and glory.

The mystery of our earthly union which Paul the apostle spoke concerning is the kind of love God has for us. With God, it is all about family. If we miss the concept of family, we miss the concept of the kingdom. We must grasp the concept of family, as it is in direct correlation with the kingdom of God. As we have laid out previously, we are "of the household of God," while we are mostly sons, God prefers lovers. Jesus is returning for a bride, not a son. The world is waiting for the manifestation of sons, but God is looking for lovers (2 Chronicles 16:9). It's always been about the heart with God. He knows that anyone can speak, but the heart earns the right to be heard. "My son, give me your heart" (Proverbs 23:26).

When a woman gives her heart to a man and he accepts it, a covenant is established, whether written or not; they have committed their affections and souls to each other. What God wants is our heart, not just our words. If he has our hearts, then he can trust us with the world around us. God had Abraham's heart, and he willed the world to Abraham. We are heirs of this inheritance, though it may not be the world of land; it may be the world of business, influence, ideas, entertainment, sports, or government. God did exploits with lovers, and he still seeks for the heart of men. "I love those who love me, and those who seek me find me. With me are riches and honor, enduring wealth and prosperity" (Proverbs 8:17–18). "For whoever finds me finds life and receives favor from the LORD" (Proverbs 8:35).

The Rich Young Ruler

The heart of man is what God is after, not perfection. Throughout the scriptures you find that God used people we ordinarily will not consider based on their history; but God is willing to invest in a person who is zealous for what they believe to be true because they want him. Let's look at a good example of the heart, **The Rich Young Ruler**. Luke 18:18–23 (KJV):

And a certain ruler asked him, saying, Good Master, what shall I do to inherit eternal life?

Interpretation: We know that Jesus is eternal life; so in other words, he was saying, what can I do to have you.

And Jesus said unto him, Why callest thou me good? none is good, save one, that is, God.

Interpretation: Herein lies the test. Remember, no one can know God except he be revealed. Jesus wanted to know if he recognized who he was; He was searching for revelation. "to whom is the arm of the lord revealed" (Isaiah 53:1). God always searches for knowledge, it is why faith need only be as small as a mustard seed to move mountains. Mustard seed faith offers invitation and opportunity. But as we know, he missed the opportunity by presenting the law. Here was grace (Jesus, the eternal life) and he chose law (works, self-righteousness) as such, Jesus gave him the law without revelation .

Thou knowest the commandments, Do not commit adultery, Do not kill, Do not steal, Do not bear false witness, Honor thy father and thy mother.

Interpretation: Jesus' response to the ruler was unmistakable. He responds by giving him the law. But wait! Jesus only gave him the last five commandments which had nothing to do with the Father. The first five commandments relate to God, and the last five to man. He did not recognize that there was more to the law he so proudly knew. A lack of knowledge puts anyone at a disadvantage. Remember, "For he that hath, to him shall be given: and he that hath not, from him shall be taken even that which he hath" (Mark 4:25 KJV).

"All these have I kept from my youth up".

Interpretation: Not only was he blinded by his self-righteous efforts—of which Jesus never disputed his claim— he did not recognize that he had no true knowledge of the Lawgiver. He kept the law, but rejected the One who wrote it. He did not have a relationship, so though he was asking for eternal life, he did not know Eternal life was before him.

Now when Jesus heard these things, he said unto him, Yet lackest thou one thing: sell all that thou hast, and distribute unto the poor, and thou shalt have treasure in heaven: and come, follow me.

Be honest with yourself, do you prefer form—an established method of procedure, over encounter? Even when the very Life he requested was before him, he did not discern it because he preferred principles rather than the knowledge that brings experience.

The true test of his heart was revealed when Jesus asked him to follow. Did he want Jesus? Was following Jesus going to be as profitable as what he has been able to acquire by following the principles of the law? Is Jesus as valuable as the possessions he had? Did he recognize that the answer to his greatest need was within reach? We are all tested on these very significant questions, and often the answers to our needs are within reach at that very moment. The challenge is, how would you respond?

The story lets us know that "Jesus looking at him, loved him". Riches can be deceiving and can sometimes blind our hearts to our greatest need. You may have heard the phrase "all that glitters is not gold"—so was the case for this "Christian"(The rich young ruler). He went to church, liked the sermons, followed the steps, but fell short of an encounter. Jesus gave him an invitation to experience with him, but he was disheartened at the thought of giving up his great possessions for the unknown—or so he thought. All the while, Jesus simply wanted to know if the ruler found him worth chasing after.

Jesus wants our love, our heart, and our affection. He wants to know if we find him worth chasing after, not merely in words, but in actions. This is what makes the Devil the most jealous; when God's people proclaim their love and also back it up with godly actions. We were created for the display of his glory. He wants to be loved by you.

Spiritual Realities

You are the glory of God! Yes, as the wife is the glory of her husband, so is the bride the glory of God. The question is, are you betrothed to him? Greater glory speaks of a realm in God—the marriage dimension. Jesus said he has given us the glory which God the Father gave him. That glory speaks of oneness—only found in the marriage covenant.

If you are called to be in business, then be a businessman or -woman. The idea is not that you cannot be more than one thing at a time, but that you **be** who

God has called you to be. When you begin with that premise, you are authentic and therefore glorious. All that God created is to bring glory to him and by doing what you were created to be, you bring him glory. Jesus brought glory to the Father by doing what God sent him to do. The trees, the birds, and the flowers all sing of God's glory when they bloom, sing, or reproduce. "I have brought you glory on earth by completing the work you gave me to do" (John 17:4). So also we are to do what he made us to do. If business, then hard work is a must because God believes in diligence and excellence, because God is excellent at what he does.

God has entrusted us to rebuild old waste places. He has given us the authority to act on his behalf—we must represent him well. We are no longer slaves in bondage to the law but heirs of the kingdom. The days of begging God to do something are over; this is the dispensation of declarations and being. We take what God has said to us—not our neighbor. We do what God says we should, not the generic word for everyone, but the word we receive from his mouth and walk on that. Everyone have been created to accomplish something. We each have our own path—take yours! Then exploits are guaranteed because his Word is truth.

Here is an example of why the Word is vital:

Walking on water. Did Peter really walk on the water? At first glance that may prove true, but a second look, ok, third; or fourth, -after meditating on it, you find that Peter was not necessarily walking on water; but rather, Peter walked on the word. "If it is you, bid me come," Peter said. And Jesus said, "Come" (Matthew 14:29–29). If Peter had jumped out of that boat without the word "Come," he would have sunk from the onset, which is why the moment he thought he was walking on water he began to sink. Another lesson in this story is this: You cannot walk on Peter's word, you must walk on the words Jesus gives you. Sometimes people try to do something someone else is doing because they are successful at it. It's their word; if you walk on someone else's word, you may sink. We all have our path in life, so receive the word from his mouth and walk on that.

Our knowledge of God determines our access to spiritual realities, the inheritance we possess, the confidence and boldness we need to operate in divine purpose. We have all been given a purpose and a destiny to fulfill on earth, but without insight we stand the chance of missing the mark. Success in life is simply this: doing what we were created to do. A manufacturer is only successful when its product functions at the level the manufacturer intended for it. God is the manufacturer; Jesus accomplished God's plan and gave us agency to accomplish ours.

However we choose to define success, it is not determined by how much money, influence, or power we have, how good of a leader we become. Though these are wonderful expressions of God's blessings, true success is coming into your fullest potential with all that God has made available to you.

Falling in love with Jesus is the best way to access this knowledge. Many want God for material needs—what can you do for me. They base their relationship with God on a professional level, often unaware of it. But God delights in giving good things to his children: he gave it all when he gave Jesus. The reason he wants us to come to him is so that we can understand what he has made available. But he will not give himself to just anyone. He wants to be wanted. He wants an invitation to unveil himself is to you.

The one who loves me will be loved by my Father, and I too will love them and show(manifest) myself to them -- John 14:21 NIV11.

When you are in love, you can do anything for the one you love. It affects every aspect of your being: how you think, sleep, eat, and even breathe. Love takes on a life of its own; you see only positives because you are taken by love. In the same way the love of God sets us on a course that has only one outcome: good success.

The Consummate Man

There are many aspects of God's love that cannot be fully expressed, they simply must be experienced, not only in feeling, but in commitment. Just like it takes a deeper level of intimacy for two individuals to become one, so it requires a deeper level of intimacy to come to the realm of oneness with Jesus, where you become one with the Father. Jesus said, "I and the Father are one" (John 10:30). This statement speaks of a **koinoniah** (Greek, for fellowship), a oneness, where two are so intimate they talk the same, walk the same, behave the same—they are inseparable. Not that they are two with the same views or characteristics, but the two come together to become one person. Jesus said he only did what he saw the Father doing, so they were in sync with one another. You ask, is this possible? "With God all things are possible". If it were not so, Jesus wouldn't have prayed that we be one with the Father, as he is (John 17:21).

Paul reaching this culmination said: "I am crucified with Christ: nevertheless I live; yet not I, but Christ liveth in me: and the life which I now live in the flesh I live by the faith of the Son of God, who loved me, and gave himself for me" (Galatians 2:20 KJV) Observe that he did not generalize it by saying we are crucified with Christ—No! He had gotten to the end of himself and had become a participant in the new one. The man had come to a place where he was inseparable from Christ, he had become the consummate man! And through the ministry of Paul we have some of the greatest knowledge on the mysteries of redemption

People love many different things, but certified lovers enjoy the flow of their lover's benefits. The secret place is a place of intimacy—just you and God in fellowship. It's a place where you are fully known—he sees you perfect! In the secret place you are holy without flaw. Why, because He is there. His radiance is more than enough to consume all imperfections. The fire of love destroys depression, disease, poverty, sickness, and imperfections. There is safety, security, friendship, trust, honor, wealth, and longevity in the secret place. In the secret place there is no death.

He that dwelleth in the secret place of the most High shall abide under the shadow of the Almighty. I will say of the LORD, He is my refuge and my fortress: my God; in him will I trust. Surely he shall deliver thee from the snare of the fowler, and from the noisome pestilence. He shall cover thee with his feathers, and under his wings shalt thou trust: his truth shall be thy shield and buckler. Thou shalt not be afraid for the terror by night; nor for the arrow that flieth by day; Nor for the pestilence that walketh in darkness; nor for the destruction that wasteth at noonday. A thousand shall fall at thy side, and ten thousand at thy right hand; but it shall not come nigh thee. Only with thine eyes shalt thou behold and see the reward of the wicked. Because thou hast made the

LORD, which is my refuge, even the most High, thy habitation; There shall no evil befall thee, neither shall any plague come nigh thy dwelling. For he shall give his angels charge over thee, to keep thee in all thy ways. They shall bear thee up in their hands, lest thou dash thy foot against a stone. Thou shalt tread upon the lion and adder: the young lion and the dragon shalt thou trample under feet. Because he hath set his love upon me, therefore will I deliver him: I will set him on high, because he hath known my name. He shall call upon me, and I will answer him: I will be with him in trouble; I will deliver him, and honor him. With long life will I satisfy him, and shew him my salvation. —Psalm 91 (KJV)

Notes:

_____

_____

_____

_____

_____

_____

Process Leads to Completion

CHAPTER 7

The Depth of Love

"And to know the love of God, which surpasses all understanding that ye might be filled with all the fullness of Gog." – Ephesians 3:19

God set out to let us know the depth of his love when he gave Jesus as the propitiation for sin. Pause and think about it! Do you know who he was? Jesus the Word, who was in God, was made flesh—that is, he came out of God; Scripture says he was the image of the invisible God, God in the flesh. He gave himself as a sacrifice for our sins. Why? That's the extent he was willing to go to have you. Jesus said, "Greater love has no one than this, that he lay down his life for his friends" (John 15:13). The greatest display of love is not the one in which we send others to give on our behalf, but the act we display ourselves. He gave himself as a sacrifice just to be with us. He doesn't want this love to simply be theoretical, he wants it to be experienced—for us to partake of it.

A similar scripture in Isaiah 53:10 further expresses the depth of this love: "it was the Lord's will to crush him," that is, Jesus. A different translation says, "it pleased the LORD to bruise him" (KJV). How could it possibly be pleasing to endure humiliation, scourging, and ultimately the cross— death—unless there was a prize worth dying for? And why did he choose this method? It was love on display, a love that is completely selfless and willing to risk it all, it was Justice. God's love that does not demand, but rather presents, and offers invitation. Hebrews 12:2 says, "who for the joy set before him endured the cross..." The prize was the joy of restoring you to your original position in God—son of the Most High, partaker of his divinity, and the object of his affection. Jesus paid the ultimate price just to have you. This is AWESOME!

The measure of God's love is found in the instruction Apostle Paul gives wives and husbands in Ephesians 5 :22 – 33.. Most Christians are unaware of the extent of God's love for them. To live unaware that God wants you, that he actually came looking for you, is to miss the key part of salvation. To discover this truth however, is to live ratified!

If you ever wanted to know how much God loves you, it is clearly, unequivocally, without any ambiguity, as much as he loves HIMSELF. WOW! Yes, God loves you as Himself—now that's mind blowing, considering the nature, splendor, and greatness of this God. His radiance is that of an unapproachable light, the Bible says: His countenance is brighter than the noonday sun in all its strength. He dwells in the third heaven where the streets are made of gold and every precious and fiery stone is laid. He is from a dateless past unto a dateless future (that is, everlasting). Yet Paul writes of a mystery concerning Christ and the church. If Jesus is our Bridegroom and we are his bride, marriage holds a key illustration into the depth of God's love.

Husbands ought also to love their own wives as their own bodies. He who loves his own wife loves himself; for no one ever hated his own flesh, but nourishes and cherishes it, just as Christ also does the church. — Ephesians 5:28–29 (NASB)

God cherishes us, as a bridegroom his bride. He rejoices over us. Heaven is cheering for us, and in that is the endorsement to live boldly and undaunted. Remember, the husband washes the bride, and presents her to himself without spot or wrinkle, holy and blameless—this is Grace! (Ephesians 5:26).

For this cause shall a man leave his father and mother, and shall be joined to his wife; and they two shall be one flesh. —Ephesians 5:31

The natural response for anyone who is greatly

loved, is to love in response. The scripture above calls for a transition, to leave one level for another; to leave something good for something better. We are greatly loved; love ought to be our response. David, the man after God's heart, said: "O Lord, you have searched me and you know me." Does God know you? Do you feel free to let him do some searching? God wants you to be real with him. He wants to know the real you; not the one you want him or people to believe you are. But he wants people who have their hearts open before Him, to let him in on what they think, and how they truly feel concerning any issue. Not because he doesn't already know, He knows what we need before we ask the bible says, yet he will not circumvent our authority or willingness to let him in. He wants us to want his involvement in all aspects of our lives. The truth is, it is He who justifies. Once you belong to him, he never points back to your flaws. He is not the accuser, instead he goes ahead of you overlooking the present, he sees who he has made you, into your future, and presents the justified you (He convicts the believer of righteousness not of sin). The only question is, do you see what he sees? If you can see it, the tendency is to move in the direction of becoming who he has made you to be—like Jesus.

You must see yourself, the way God sees you in the Spirit, it is from that level you can authentically join in with what heaven is declaring.

Jesus was in total surrender to the will of the Father in mind, body, and spirit. Though he was the full embodiment of the God head, Jesus was also fully man in total oneness with God. He was given the Holy Spirit without measure. In the same way, God wants us united to him. As Christians, we will never experience the depth of God's love or experience the abundant life (John 10:10) that he came to give without the intentional effort to *know* him. It is in the journey of discovering who he is, we find out who we are.

Beholding God's Glory

"When I consider your heavens, the work of your fingers, the moon and the stars, which you have set in place, what is man that you are mindful of him, the son of man that you care for him?" Psalm 8:3–4

It is said that the question of Psalm 8:4 was taking place in the heavens rather than here on earth. David was not kicking back, gazing at the moon and the stars, marveling at God's galactic power. But rather, he was having a revelation of what took place in the heavens after man came on the scene. Perhaps, this was the response of angelic beings in astonishment as to why God vested so much of his heart on this particular creation. Though not proven, it makes sense. The one who created all things, the wonder of the universe, who set the stars in place with his fingers. The one who created the mighty cherubim and seraphim angels, and the host of heavenly beings, who formed thousands of galaxies that cluster together, and the billions of stars that inhabit them— get the picture? There was great wonder in the heavens for the creation called man.

The great amazement was the affection with which he created this particular creature, man. Granted, God loves all that he created, but there was none like the one whom he touched. His passion, focus, and affection toward man as the angels gazed in awe was remarkable. His delight was with mankind (Proverbs 8:31). So, as you take this journey into the depths of love, consider the work of his hands, allow it to give you access into the knowledge of him and his great love for you!

The manifested glory of God upon a persons life is a result of proximity. How close are you? Yes, we are saved and justified when we become born again, but the level of glory we possess is a direct result of knowing him, that is, experiencing his person. God's glory is ever changing; it becomes more radiant as you behold him. When we come into the presence of God, his glory extends toward us. Because his glory is always greater than the last, we also go from glory to glory as a result of the greater glory we behold – there is always more of him to *know*.

The Bible gives us a picture of this changing glory in the

book of Revelation: the twenty-four elders who worshipped before the throne of God. They came and bowed before him who sat on the throne. And every time they raised their heads to behold him, his glory intensified, which all the more caused them to bow and worship even more, and so they fell to their knees again and again and again as a result of the intensifying glory, a glory in constant intensity for eternity. So also, when we are in intimate fellowship with the Lord, we become more and more glorious as we behold him.

"and we all, with unveiled face, continually seeing as in a mirror the glory of the Lord, are progressively being transformed into His image from [one degree of] glory to [even more] glory…" – 2 Cor 3:18.

Further Study:

What do you see/know or understand better of God that you didn't otherwise see before?

_____

_____

_____

_____

_____

_____

_____

_____

_____

_____

Faith expresses itself through Love

CHAPTER 8

God Wants Your Love

"For the eyes of the LORD run to and fro throughout the whole earth, to show himself strong in the behalf of them whose hearts is perfect toward him."
- 2 Chronicles 16:9 KJV

Long before we knew God, he had already set his affection on us. He is always the initiator of the process. He knows that if he can get our attention and get us to taste of his goodness, we cannot refuse him. He is completely irresistible! He is flawless in nature and character, he is all together lovely, he is the fairest among ten thousand, meaning in every set of ten thousand among ten thousand, he is more beautiful to behold. He said to Moses at Mount Sinai, "I will cause all my goodness to pass in front of you" (Exodus 33:19). Now that's a way to get attention. His goodness on display causes men to stop for transformation and direction.

God has honored us with the invitation to know him and love him. He wants to be loved by you not because he needs it to be who he is, or because there is something lacking in him. A thousand times NO. In loving him we are transformed and blessed—we partake of his love and divine nature. We become like the one we worship. His presence becomes something you crave, like the most awesome addiction. Your soul, even your flesh, wants him, to feel the tangible embrace of his presence, because you have tasted the sweetest of loves.

Failure-Proof

Love gives us the permission to become a sign and a wonder on the earth. The Bible says, "God is love; and he that dwells in love dwells in God" (1 John AKJV). Love is a person! Think of it for a moment: to dwell in God, that is, to live in him and for him to live in you. What would you do with your life if you knew that God loved you beyond all doubt? That his love shields you from the enemy? Who would you be, if you knew Love, and loved Love the same way? When you give God the right of way in your life, he will cause you to ride on the waves of life.

Scripture is loaded with the promises of God to those who love him. Love undoubtedly holds the key to hidden treasures. What is true in Deuteronomy 6:5, Psalms 91, Proverbs 8:17, 2 Chronicles 7:14, and Matthew 6:33 guarantees a failure-proof life. Until you truly know that you are loved, you will not make a success of your life. Until a wife knows her husband undoubtedly loves her, she would lack the confidence needed to establish her dominion in her home; she will not be settled in her heart and, therefore, that home may not be on a sure foundation. Likewise, until a husband knows his wife loves him, he would not be settled in his heart and may lack the focus and confidence he needs to lead his family. Children have to know that they are loved. Love is a language. Love speaks. Until you *know* God's love, you cannot love. When you understand that God loves you, you understand that God wants you. Then you understand that he cares for you and has a specific purpose for you.

You have heard the scripture "love never fails" (1 Corinthians 13:8). This is because love is the highest currency by which God trades and wants us to trade by. Sermons often point to faith as the currency of the kingdom. Let's refocus that belief although true: faith works by love (Galatians 5:6), which we will deal with in the chapters to come. Keep in mind that in every act of faith we see in the Bible, Jesus, the substance, is what is in focus and not the evidence. The woman with the issue of blood in Luke's gospel touched the hem of his garment and was made whole. Whatever knowledge she had of Jesus convinced her that he was worth going after in spite of the risk. Jesus was the substance, her healing was the evidence of her faith. Go for the substance, and the evidence will manifest.

After God's Heart

Many seek after things, riches, fame, popularity, and men's approval. Many also seek after God, but not for the genuine purpose of knowing him, but rather for what they can get from him. David was considered a man after God's heart, and his love for God's presence earned him a place in eternity. To be after God's heart is an adventure. It's a quest to know him, and experience him, and take hold of him. To know his heart is to know what makes him happy or sad, what he loves or hates, what he wants, his nature, his presence, and his justice.

To be after God's heart is the will of God, and a man at the center of God's will is immortal until his assignment is over. Love makes the lover incapable of being destroyed, ruined, or rendered ineffective. Consider the three Hebrew boys in the book of Daniel: Hananiah, Mishael, and Azariah (Shadrach, Meshach and Abednego). They showed the dedication of their love by not eating the king's meat or bowing to the king's idol, and because love never fails, Love showed up in the fiery furnace (Daniel 3).

Consider King David, a man after God's heart: "I will

allow no sleep to my eyes, no slumber to my eyelids, till I find a place for the LORD, a dwelling for the Mighty One of Jacob" (Psalm 132:4–5).

David's love for God gave him unrest that the ark of God's covenant had no resting place. The ark of covenant was a representation of God's presence among his people, and David's heart could not bear to the separation. A heart for God gives him a place of preeminence, honor, reverence, glory, thanksgiving, and praise. King David is proof that love is eternal. Notice that Jesus is called "the Son of David." Today we read in Revelation 3:7 and 5:5 that Jesus has the key of David and is the Root of David. Love made David irreplaceable for all eternity. David was so in tune with the heart of God he knew how God, and God knew him. David knew how to stir the heart of God, he knew what gets God to respond even when he otherwise would not have—now that's big!

"May they who love you be like the sun when it rises in its strength" (Judges 5:31).

Please understand that this kind of love begins with your knowledge of God's love for you. God had already proved his love to Hananiah, Mishael, and Azariah, as well as David, they had deep knowledge with encounter. Since they knew he was with them, they had come to a place where all doubt of God's love and faithfulness had been dismissed.

God first loved us (1 John 4:10). In the Old Testament, God proved his love by signs and wonders—not that we don't have them today, but because Jesus had not yet come, he showed his love by the prophets, destroying the enemies of Israel before them. He has proven his love again and again by giving us Jesus, and after Jesus left, he gave us His Holy Spirit. Pursue the knowledge of him, there is success in his love. When you really come to know by revelation how much God loves you, you are set on your course for exploits.

Whatever your place or position in life, you were born to reign. Jesus Christ died for that purpose to make you a king and a priest – act like it! Study kings and exercise your priestly duties. You have the life of God in you and that life cannot die; it is eternal. Sickness and disease, sin and despair, curses and poverty, shame and ignorance, you reign over the decadence of this world. Your ability to reign in this life is contingent on how far your eyes can see: that is, the eyes of your understanding.

Further Study

Read the book of Deuteronomy chapter 10: 8-9, 12 - 13.

The duties of the Levites (Priests)

_____
_____
_____
_____
_____
_____

Do you recognize what God truly wants to give you?

_____
_____
_____
_____
_____

Process enables you to Become

CHAPTER 9

The More Excellent Way

Now eagerly desire the greater gifts. And yet I will show you the most excellent way... - **1 Corinthians12:31(NIV)**

At first glance, one might think that 1 Corinthians 13, 4 through 7 is a quality for believers to possess. Love is...but looking closely you find that it is more of a description than instruction. It describes a person, one we are to get to know, not something we try to achieve. Think of it: "if I speak in the tongues of men or of angels, but do not have love...If I have the gift of prophesy and can fathom all mysteries and all knowledge... but do not have love, I gain nothing" (1 Corinthians 13:1–3 NIV11). The writer of this letter, Paul, is trying to invite the reader into encounter. This scripture is not to the unbeliever but to those who believe. It is an invitation to lay hold of the person called Love.

You can be a believer, yet have no hold on God. Listen, we are called to something much more than memorized scripture or religious morals. We have been called to lay hold of a Holy God, and never let go (Song of Songs 3:4).

Our high calling is a call to unity and fellowship with our creator, to know (epignosis) him, and love him. The reason many fail in their quest to try to love others is because the sequence is often out of place. It is in knowing him, receiving his love and loving him, that we can then love others. When you know how much He loves you, you can begin to love yourself, and others. You can't love others if you don't know how to truly love you.

The high call of God is not to become a preacher, evangelist, apostle, or prophet. It is a call to search Him out personally. It is for us to know our truest identity, without encounter, we cannot really we cannot take hold of him. Just as parents derive joy from their child's discovery of Santa gifts on Christmas morning, God takes great pleasure in our discovery of all he has so freely made available to us. You have heard the phrase, "there is no high like the Most High."

Well, David said it best in Psalm 34:9, "Oh taste and see that the LORD is good" (NKJV). He lets us taste—

invitation— then we see—experience. But he searches, oh he searches the hearts of men for the slightest hint of reception. He wants to know that we want him. He is unobtrusive, and will only come by invitation. The Lord searched David's heart and many others in the Old Testament, Jesus searched in the New Testament, and the Holy Spirit is still searching!

"I have found David my servant; with my holy oil have I anointed him" (Psalm 89:20 KJV). The Bible says the prophet Samuel went to the house of Jesse to anoint a new king for Israel, but God stopped Samuel as he was about to anoint the first born of Jesse: "But the LORD said to Samuel, 'Don't judge by his appearance or height, for I have rejected him.' The LORD doesn't see things the way you see them. People judge by outward appearance, but the LORD looks at the heart" (1 Samuel 16:7 NLT).

"I have rejected him"? So he had considered him, and found him unacceptable. To be rejected, you have to first be considered. Therefore the condition of your heart toward him would determine how close you get to taking hold of him. What he wants is not our charity, religious association, prophesy, tongues, or even faith. Yes, not even faith. So many try and often fail to conjure up faith. Because faith apart from Jesus is ineffective— faith works by love, and God who is Love is the author of it. So you see why many get frustrated and confused. Great faith is a by-product of an awareness of who Jesus really is. He wants an authentic heart, a heart that sees him and recognizes he is the answer— that He is enough!

"And now these three remain: faith, hope and love. But the greatest of these is love" (1 Corinthians 13:13).

Love "always trusts"! As though this were humanly possible. We can't always trust. But when we realize that God is speaking of himself, we can then be affected by what we behold of him. People we love will fail us many times, so why would God ask us to always trust people? That actually contradicts Psalm 118:8, which says, "It is better to take refuge in the LORD than to trust in man" (NASB). But as the Holy Spirit becomes your teacher, you become aware that this speaks of the character of God. He can always be trusted.

"Love keeps no record of wrong," this is God's nature and how he sees us. He sees you in perfection. Love then, is not a law to practice simply for the sake of it, but rather, these are the attributes of God. It's the same theme of the Old Testament commandment (10 commandments). When Moses received the law of God, it was not so much an instruction to him, but a revelation of Gods nature and character. To lay hold of his nature and character is the key to understanding who we are to become. The bible says, " as we behold him we are transformed". You got to see before you can become.

When Perfection Comes

"But when perfection comes, the imperfect disappears"
(1 Corinthians 13:10).

When you lay hold of God, all your imperfections disappear. If you have received Christ as lord over your life, you have been made perfect; so never see yourself as unholy. You may do unholy things and have impure thoughts, but the truth is your old nature has been killed and buried. Your responsibility is to put to death the carnal nature and keep it from rising up in you. God always works with truth not facts. The ideal you from a natural perspective has some flaws—ok, a lot of flaws, but God sees you from a supreme perspective. In God's leadership style, He works from knowledge, to revelation, into experience. Inside Out! So he reaches into the future and shows you who you are, then you learn to become what he sees when looks at you. You have been justified and that helps us get a picture of who we are suppose to become – Christ-like!

If there is anything we must know about God, it is this: He is a God of knowledge. He does not want us doing things out of ignorance. As a matter of fact, God has waited for the age of knowledge to pour out deep revelation on scripture, just so we could have the capacity to receive the blessing.

Many people want instant impartation, they want magic, and it does them no good but lead to deception and manipulation. You cannot remove God from process. God will always take us through process in other to refine us.

Further Reading:

Jesus made it clear in Matthew 6:33—seek first the kingdom and his righteousness and he will allot you your portion with great rewards.

_____

_____

_____

Contend to have him first and not what is in his hands. He is healing, he is wealth, he is every good thing we can desire, and we are bound to have true riches when we have him. The secret is really no secret at all.

_____

_____

_____

Proverbs 8:17–19, 21: "I love those who love me, and those who seeks me find me. "With me are riches and honor, enduring wealth and prosperity. My fruit is better than fine gold; what I yield surpasses choice silver...Bestowing wealth on those who love me and making their treasuries full." With the above scriptures, who needs more explanation on the rewards of having him?

_____

_____

_____

_____

_____

_____

The Process is From Victory

CHAPTER 10

The Counter-Balance of Grace

"But the world must learn that I love the Father and that I do exactly what my Father has commanded me" —John 14:31

It is time for us the church, to show proofs of what we believe! As the saying goes, "the proof is in the pudding." It is not enough to boast about one's cooking abilities, it is in the eating the result speaks for itself. This is the time to move from speaking to doing. Anyone can speak, but we earn the right to be heard. That right is earned by your proofs—what you do! The kingdom of God is not limited to the four walls of a building. Granted, church buildings are fellowship centers for refueling, confirmation, and impartation, but the kingdom of God is in you to do the work of God.

We must be the change we want to see on earth. Time is now of the essence. Whatever your hand finds to do for the kingdom, do it with your might. Love people. Help people. Live generously. The world must see the difference in the believer. God gave you an assignment, a dream, a talent, a responsibility, and a command; doing it is how you prove you love him.

Love also has to do with trust. You cannot fully obey someone you do not trust. It's like a loving father telling his mature son to jump—I'll catch you—and the son hesitates to do so. His hesitation proves there is some lack of trust, either he has not been perfected in his father's love or he just doubts his father's ability, he may fear that his dad might make a mistake and let him fall. Nonetheless, his knowledge of his father's love for him has not been perfected; he needs a revelation of who his father really is, and an understanding of his father's love and what his father means when he says he loves his son. Normally, because our earthly fathers love us, they provide, they protect, they defend, and they empower. How much more the love of God?

Proofs

Jesus had to prove his love for the Father by doing his work. What makes you think you get a free ride? Please don't misunderstand this statement, the doing here does not refer to Salvation. Salvation is by pure grace, and we are in constant need to be reminded of his great love. The message of grace is to let us know that by no effort of ours do we deserve the inheritance God has so richly given us. Grace is truly unmerited.

But we have work to do. The enemy gains advantage over us when we go to the extreme of the truth God reveals to us; we must always have the right balance—a correct weight (Proverbs 11:1, 20:23). When we talk about works, we are not referring to works of the law that try to obtain righteousness by doing righteous deeds (self-righteousness). NO, a thousand times no! We are made righteous through the work of the cross and that alone. However, we have been recreated to do righteous deeds because we have been made righteous. Jesus said "I must do the work of him who sent me" (John 9:4 ISV). Likewise, we also must do the work he created us to do: establishing dominion all over the earth, taking territories, enforcing kingdom principles, and ruling in the sphere of influence God gives us.

All Hands on Deck

We are to come completely out of obscurity and let our voices be heard. Not in the manner that some have chosen and therefore portrayed intolerance and hate, but with love and understanding, knowing that it is the grace of God that leads people to repentance. The world must see our works. The people of God have been doing great things for a long time, but we chose to live by the statement Jesus made addressing giving: "So when you give to the needy, do not announce it with trumpets, as the hypocrites do in the synagogues and on the streets, to be honored by others. Truly I tell you, they have received their reward in full. But when you give to the needy, do not let your left hand know what your right hand is doing, so that your giving may be in secret" (Matthew 6:2–4 NIV11).

Taken in context, Jesus was not saying the world around them could not know what they were doing to help the poor. He simply meant, if you are doing it to show how good you are (self-righteousness) or for the praise of men, then you are being a hypocrite; it is the condition of the heart. So then, as lovers of God, we must let the light he gives us shine for all to see. By doing so, we inspire others to follow.

"As we let our own light shine, we unconsciously give other people permission to do the same." Marianne Williamson, "A Return to Love".

We live in the media age, and the world is taking full advantage of every form of media there is to spread the message of superficial love. We have the love of God; it's time we spread it across the earth. When the world sees our works, the companies we run with excellence, the helps we render to those near and far, the excellence of our character, and the discipline of our actions, they will know we are a peculiar people. We must begin to do the works prepared for us to do: rebuilding old waste places, expelling darkness, and releasing more of heaven on the earth.

Every son of God has heaven inside him (both male and female, we are all sons of God), that is why "the earnest expectation of the creature waits for the manifestation of the sons [huios] of God" (Roman 8:19 KJV). Creation is waiting for you to manifest your God-given gifts, talents, and abilities. Everyone is called in some capacity to do something for the advancement of the kingdom. We are to stop the world around us from decay.

Note:

_____

_____

_____

_____

_____

The Process of God

Process Keeps You in Balance

CHAPTER 11

The Counter-Balance of Love

"For we must all before the judgment seat of Christ, that each one may receive what is due him for the things done while in the body, whether good or bad." - 2 Corinthians 5:10

The counter-balance of love, is The Fear of the Lord, which is obedience to instruction. Grace is not the indirect permission to sin; but rather, it is the enabling power to be a doer of the word. But first, let's make this distinction. God loves those who belong to him, even those who don't know him yet. He is passionately in-love with those who have been born of the Spirit. However, there is also a fierce side to God, He is a God that kills. He is a consuming fire! All who fight against him or hate him will always experience the Lion of the Tribe of Judah__ Dead! Search the scriptures all his enemies are destroyed. "All you hate me, love death" (Proverbs 8:36).

Now that we've gotten that out of the way, let's explore the balance of God's love for those that belong to Him.

Proverbs 16:6 (KJV) says, "by the fear of the LORD men depart from evil," which will never change no matter how much grace you've been given. In the church today, the topic of holiness is unpopular and considered a turn-off. There is no Christianity without holiness, a Holy Man died that we might through his blood become holy. We only need to live out what grace has deposited. Grace empowers us to live out the righteous life. If you are struggling with an area in your life, what you need is the experiential knowledge of God's grace in that area. If you find out how much he loves you, by encounter, sin will not have dominion over you (paraphrasing Romans 6:14) because now you know, and you love him too.

It is always grace and truth; this strikes the balance. If we only choose grace without truth, we will live a lie. If we choose truth alone without grace, we become judgmental. God detests an unjust scale as far as his Word is concerned. Jesus said, "If you love me, you will obey me" (John 14:23, paraphrased). In other words, when you love me, you will do what pleases me. You cannot know him without loving him.

Wisdom is the principal thing and the fear of the Lord is the beginning of wisdom (Proverbs 9:10). So having the fear of the Lord is greatly rewarding.

"The fear of the LORD is pure, enduring forever."—Psalm 19:9

The fear of God helps us to exercise courage, courage to be holy in a world full of sin and moral decay. The courage to want more of him. Actually the words "fear not" or "be not afraid" appear many times in the Scriptures. Fear keeps us from the possibility of experiencing change. The Fear of the Lord is not as we would naturally understand fear. Psalm 19:9 says the fear of the Lord is pure (unpolluted) and endures forever. The fear of the Lord is not just reverential fear—to show great honor, respect, and adoration with fear. Those are by- products of knowing the value to whom this gesture is bestowed. If you come before an earthly king without properly acknowledging and addressing him, chances are you are not going to be heard, much less get your request granted.

The fear of the Lord and the love of the Lord are interrelated. You can't revere a person you have not already determined is worthy of it. Therefore, having the fear of the Lord takes some knowledge. Throughout Scripture, the fear of the Lord is always tied to the presence of a person—the person of the Holy Spirit. In the days of old, God gave his Spirit so that his people Israel would fear him. Not a fear to dread him or run from him, but a fear to want him more and not want to be apart from him. Think of it! Not wanting to be separate from God. Now that's an awesome fear—bring it on!

Jesus delighted in the fear of the Lord because he was constantly in the Father's presence. Abiding in the presence of God and greater works go together because it is the enabling force that helps us carry out the instructions of God. You can't obey God without being empowered or enabled. Hence, you never find the fear of the Lord without a call to obedience. So not only is the fear of the Lord obedience to instruction, the fear of the Lord is dreading his absence.

Let's examine some of the major giants in the Bible who were noted for the fear of the Lord:

We start with Abraham, the father of faith. He was to give his "only" son (son of promise) as a sacrifice to the Lord. An angel of the Lord appeared to him and said "Do not stretch out your hand against the lad, and do nothing to him; for now I know that you fear God" (Genesis 22:12 NASB).

Joseph feared God: "There is none greater in this house than I; neither hath he kept back anything from me but thee, because thou art his wife: how then can I do this great wickedness, and sin against God?" (Genesis 39:9

KJV).

Moses: "Friend of God." "If your Presence does not go with us, do not send us up from here" (Exodus 33:15 NIV).

David: A man after God's heart. "Do not cast me from your presence or take your Holy Spirit from me." (Psalm 51:11)

Job: A man who feared God and avoided evil. "Oh, for the days when I was in my prime, when God's intimate friendship blessed my house, when the Almighty was still with me and my children were around me" (Job 29:4–5). "And this is what he says to all humanity: 'the fear of the Lord is true wisdom; to forsake evil is real understanding'" (Job 28:28 NLT).

Solomon: A man of wisdom. He concluded in Ecclesiastes: "Fear God and obey his commands, for this is everyone's duty" (12:13 NLT).

All the above-mentioned men of faith had one thing in common, they had a relationship with God, and they did as God commanded. Job said during his affliction that he longed for the days when the Almighty was his delight. This speaks of intimacy. Abraham believed God. Joseph would not sin against God. And they all had glorious ends. Not one died poor or diseased.

"The fear of the LORD is the beginning of

Wisdom"(Psalm 111:10); that is, no divine wisdom without The Fear of the Lord. Job says, "It cannot be valued with the gold of Ophir" (Job 28:16 KJV). "But where shall wisdom be found?...man knoweth not the price thereof; neither is it found in the land of the living...For the price of wisdom is above rubies...For he looketh to the ends of the earth, and seeth under the whole heaven...Then did he see it, and declare it...And unto man he said, Behold, the fear of the LORD, that is wisdom" (Job 28:12–13, 18, 24, 27 KJV). No amount of grace will ever neutralize the need for the fear of the Lord. The fear of the Lord is also a poof of love. When you love, you trust and therefore obey.

"Blessed is the man who fears the LORD, who finds great delight in his commands" (Psalm 112:1).

The fear of the Lord is key to fulfilling your purpose. You cannot do it by might. The prophet Isaiah lets us know in the thirty-third chapter that the fear of the Lord opens the door to the treasures of wisdom, knowledge, and security.

That wisdom is far better than gold and rubies. Having the fear of the Lord is to have a sure foundation and the key to great spiritual treasures.

You might be wondering how you can Do the Word with all your imperfections and short comings? This is how! Jesus said "If you love me, you will keep my words," to paraphrase John 14:15. In other words, don't worry—when you get to know me, you'll love me, then keeping my words become easier. And "if we walk in the light, as he is in the light, we have fellowship with one another, and the blood of Jesus, his Son, purifies us from all sin" (1 John 1:7). So you see, his commandments are truly not grievous, because he helps us in the ongoing process.

Obedience

"He will delight in the fear of the LORD."— Isaiah 11:3

Whoever said Grace is an excuse for disobedience has not encountered the love of God. Granted, we are not called to the letter of the law, but we are called to do the Word. Grace is about relationship, and that makes it easier to do what God commands. We are not hearers only, but rather doers also (James 1:22), otherwise there would be no need to hear in the first place. When we become children of God, we are born of the Word; so doing the Word becomes the result of our hearing.

As you grow in your relationship with the Holy Spirit, it will serve you well to study the fear of the Lord. Immerse yourself in Scriptures like Proverbs 4:7, 9:10, 16:6, and ask for understanding. Let your quest be to know what fearing him truly represents. Let your spirit gain insight into this scared fear, for it goes deeper than honor, respect, reverence, and obedience. Like hidden treasure search Isaiah 11:3. If Jesus the Son of God, who was the Word made flesh according to prophecy, delighted in the fear of the Lord, then it is necessary for victorious living and destiny.

Jesus said in John's gospel: "If you love me, you will obey what I command" (John 14:15). This is the litmus test: you know that you truly love me when you obey me. You cannot authentically love God and not obey him. No doubt his love comes first, but once you have been honored to experience his love, the Holy Spirit leads you to this holy fear. It is the kind of fear that dreads the absence of his presence. The one that cannot stand to hurt him. That carries no type of offense toward God for any reason. To esteem him higher than anyone else or anything, including you. To consider what he thinks concerning your decisions. If you love him, you are consumed by him, because he is irresistible. He occupies your heart and purifies it. God calls and is calling us into fellowship with his Son Jesus. He is calling us to our first love, whether we know it or not.

We must understand that we were created for him, for his glory. Knowledge, understanding, and surrender are the ultimate vehicles to getting into this deeper intimacy with Jesus.

Delight in him first because it is the first and only determining factor for access to God's treasure, his heart. Remember, seeking first the kingdom is actually seeking him first: he is the kingdom. He is the First and the Last, and therefore the only.

The fear of the Lord helps give us a balanced picture of grace and what it truly means to love God. We have been called into an adventure with the author of the world, to seek the knowledge of him. This knowledge (epignosis) of the Lord leads us into experience and brings understanding—and that, my friend, is wisdom.

My son, if you accept my words and store up my commands within you, turning your ear to wisdom and applying your heart to understanding, and if you call out for insight and cry aloud for understanding, and if you look for it as for silver and search for it as for hidden treasure, then you will understand the fear of the LORD and find the knowledge of God. —Proverbs 2:1–5

Further Study:
Mediate on Proverbs 2:1 -5 until you grasp what the Spirit of God is saying, then write down what comes to your heart.

_____
_____
_____
_____

Process Makes You Rich.

CHAPTER 12

They That Know Their God

But the people that do know their God shall be strong, and do exploits. **-Daniel 11:32 (KJV)**

They that know their God are crowned with glory and destined for exploits. They are the history makers, the pathfinders, the trailblazers, and the pacesetters. Though the world seems to be in turbulence, the outpouring of the knowledge of God by the Holy Spirit is making successes out of sons and daughters. The glory of the end-time church and the manifestation of the sons of God is coming in unusual packages. God is pouring out his Spirit upon all flesh, so consider the person next to you.

The mature sons of God are not trying to escape the world, but rather are establishing the kingdom on earth.

There is a shifting and a great awakening of God's manifested presence among his people. His people are beginning to live in the reality of the full life Christ has made available. It's in the way of divine relationships, in the big but also small victories and breakthroughs, the favors, and the anointing.

The sons and daughters are prophesying, declaring the word of God with boldness. The young men are seeing visions of possibilities and establishing it on the earth. The old men are dreaming, tapping into the divine realm and revealing "as it is in heaven." We are increasing in our awareness of who we are because we cannot afford to walk in these times unaware of what we have been freely given and what we possess. The veil has been lifted and therefore we see and manifest what is within. We may over the years have taken minimal risks due to ignorance, fear, and religious restrictions, but now we take our place in him, in truth.

The natural mind had been a barrier for the life of the renewed one, hence we were unprepared for the supernatural. The natural mind is religious at best, but religion keeps up appearances but lacks power or proofs. But we believe God and therefore we speak what we know, and manifest that truth, making believers of all others as Jesus did. For the kingdom of God is not only in words, it is a kingdom of power seeking expression on the earth in every sphere of society. God is bigger than what we think, so we think bigger and take risks!

Knowledge

But let the one who boasts boast about this: that they have the understanding to know me, that I am the LORD, who exercises kindness, justice and righteousness on earth, for in these I delight," declares the LORD.—Jeremiah 9:24

Before Adam and Eve sinned, they had one knowledge, the knowledge of good (God). But when they sinned against God, they gained another knowledge; the knowledge of evil. God's intention was never for creation to know the knowledge of evil, because it corrupts the soul and ultimately the spirit. Imagine creation with the knowledge of good and good alone; we would have built paradise on earth with the help of the Lord. We would have a world of constant joy, peace, and prosperity for all. After all, that's what the world is chasing after. But Jesus, "in whom are hid all the treasures of wisdom and knowledge"(Colossians 2:3 KJV), came to restore that knowledge; the awareness of him who is Good, in order that each individual may experience fellowship with God.

The knowledge of God is vital; it is the invitation to intimate fellowship and all the treasures of heaven. Too many know about him, have an awareness of him, but not too many experience him intimately. It is in knowing him we come to know our true selves, our inheritance, our position, and thereby the measure of his great love.

Jesus said to the teachers of religious law: "You study the Scriptures diligently because you think that in them you have eternal life. These are the very Scriptures that testify about me, yet you refuse to come to me to have life" (John 5:39–40 NIV11). Those religious teachers possessed intellectual knowledge but lacked awareness, which would have led them into experience with the Son of God. Likewise today, many know about God and his son Jesus Christ through observations, teachings, and human understanding, but this kind of knowledge puffs up. The ability to prove that we know something yet lack transformation, typifies the person who has religion.

> I keep asking that the God of our Lord Jesus Christ, the glorious Father, may give you the Spirit of wisdom and revelation, so that you may know him better.—Ephesians 1:17

Revelation Knowledge

Ginosko (awareness): Revelation knowledge that leads to experience. Its purpose is to unveil and take you into experience. It's the reality of friendship, where you get to know Jesus, and the eyes of your understanding begins to open up. You are able to relate with the Scriptures and find truth. Truth which comes by the

Spirit of God and not the letter of the law. "Simon Peter answered, 'You are the Christ, the Son of the living God.' And Jesus said to him, 'Blessed are you, Simon son of Jonah, because flesh and blood did not reveal this to you, but My Father who is in heaven'" (Matthew 16:16-17 NASB). Peter's knowledge came by revelation, not head knowledge.

The knowledge of God is available to all who want an encounter with him, and the beauty with the Lord is this: when you get a revelation of who he is, he tells you who you are. "I also say to you that you are Peter, and upon this rock I will build My church; and the gates of Hades will not overpower it" (Matthew 16:18 NASB).

The revelation of who God is leads to encounter, and encounter requires manifestation to validate that revelation. However the manifestation here does not come because of the revelation, but it is an invitation to explore what has been unveiled. Meaning, when you get a revelation from God, you must begin operating from that perspective, and soon the manifestation will soon start to show.

Full Knowledge

Epignosis (full or exact knowledge): True knowledge or understanding which comes out of experience and encounter, leading to full awareness of God's presence. As we have thoroughly explored, full knowledge comes by experience; everything else is in measure. **Epignosis** is a place of comprehension, grasping by apprehension thereby the revelation makes you become an active participant. This is the knowledge Paul speaks about in Ephesians 3:19 to have complete knowledge which fills a person with the fullness of God. Meaning, in whatever area of your life you receive an encounter; He comes in all his fullness. If you were sick in your body, and by encounter he heals you, you can never be sick again in that area in which he came in all his fullness. This is why Jesus could say to the one man out of the ten who were lepers, "go thy way, thy faith hath made thee whole" (Luke 17:19 KJV). The others got measure, but the one who return for encounter, got fullness.

The Place of the Mind

The mind is the most powerful constituent of the human experience. It is the natural aptitude to think for ourselves. Nothing occurs within the soul without the use of the mind; hence it is evermore necessary that our minds are exposed to the realities and possibilities available to us. We are no better than our minds. When it is all said and done, our lives would have been the sum total of our thinking process. What separates one human from another is the state of our minds.

Ever wonder why the great minds of our time are not the most religious, yet blaze trails, it is their ability to think without limits. God wants us to take the limits off our imagination. See possibilities, for this is only what heaven sees!

The mind we have been given is able to tap into what seems naturally impossible and makes it possible, because it sees what lies within. Once the mind is able to see it, it is as good as real. God does not exist simply to meet our needs. That way of thinking is for servants. While he does meet needs, he prefers that we become conduits who meet the needs of everyone around us on his behalf. This takes place with a transformed thinking when we seek the kingdom first. The kingdom of God is a heavenly reality, and the transformed mind works in conjunction with God's kingdom to manifest "on earth as it is in heaven."

The mind is either being transformed (metamorphosis) or it is at war with God; there are no neutral grounds. What he wants to give us is not money, careers, or houses. One of the greatest gifts he came to give us is a change in perspective. Things around you are not the way they are, they are the way you are. Pause! Read it again. If then our lives are a reflection of our thought patterns, we can change our lives. The question is, what do you see? We don't see things the way they are, but rather, the way we are. The uninformed mind will often always go for the subjective—instinct. But Jesus came so that we could think differently.

The renewed mind was the basis from which he taught; it was why the religious leaders of his day and often today despise the teaching of the true message of grace. Grace changes our perspective. It enables us to operate on a higher plane and illuminate the reality of a heavenly realm.

Religious Thinking

In the past, the church possessed a beggarly attitude. Thank God for illumination; we are coming out of the old ways of thinking—a religious box. Religion always seeks to limit, control, and quite frankly, enslave. Jesus died to restore the sanctity of your mind. Believers waited for manna to fall from heaven, relied on the pastor to hear what God was saying, and limited the scope of what they could be.

Most Christians are subject to poverty because they do not have a good knowledge of who God is for them, and it has persisted far longer than it ought to have. Many have died thinking suffering was a statement of humility—but that is false humility. God takes pleasure in the prosperity of his saints (Psalm 35:27). A religious mind-set will enclose you every time. Especially when it comes to the things of God. How can a poor man have dominion? Over what? A poor person cannot even have dominion over his poverty because the poverty calls the shots: "The poverty of the poor is their destruction" (Proverbs 10:15 NLT). Religion says you are being greedy when you want more than enough. The transformed mind knows it will take more than just enough to make big impact.

The religious wait, the renewed mind goes.

"Go to the ant, thou sluggard; Consider her ways, and be wise: Which having no chief, Overseer, or ruler, Provideth her bread in the summer, And gathereth her food in the harvest. How long wilt thou sleep, O sluggard? When wilt thou arise out of thy sleep? Yet a little sleep, a little slumber, A little folding of the hands to sleep: So shall thy poverty come as a robber, And thy want as an armed man" (Proverbs 6:6–11 ASV)

A renewed mind is the one that discovers God's heart for you. That means you have a new birth right as the beloved of God to know what purpose you are here to fulfill. It is impossible for you to be in Christ and not be blessed. It defies everything Jesus' sacrifice stands for. God has put you in Christ, not Christ before the cross, but the Christ after the cross. The one who is on the throne of majesty.

God has made it possible for us to explore his goodness and discover blessings. It is up to you to live life in a way that enables you to receive all the blessings he has provided for. God speaks 24/7, to whom are you tuned in? The radio stations are on all the time, but you will not hear what is being said unless you are tuned in.

Our Divine Advantage

That God wants to revolutionize your life is no cliché. It is what he set out to do since the fall of man. He wants to fundamentally change your perspective, release his presence through you on earth, and endow you with power. Power to change your world and that of others around you. But first, let me briefly present the strategist for a beautiful life on earth: the Holy Spirit. It would take an entire book just to scratch the surface of his person, so a brief presentation. The Holy Spirit is the presence of God; when God shows up in a prayer meeting, church service, or a person's life, it is by his Spirit. The Holy Spirit is God, the third person of the Trinity, not to be mistaken for a position or rank. This term has caused many to neglect the most influential person of the Trinity, relegating him to the background.

The Word of God tells us what to do, but the Holy Spirit is the one who tells us how to do it. He was the strategist in creation. When the Lord began creating the earth, it was the Holy Spirit who designed it and brought order to it (Genesis 1:2).

How Important Is the Holy Spirit?

Jesus, the eternal Son of God could do nothing

without the Holy Spirit. In fact, according to the prophet Isaiah, the Son would not take on the mission as atoning sacrifice without the guarantee of the Holy Spirit's accompaniment. He is that important! Jesus said in John 16:7: "Nevertheless I tell you the truth; It is expedient for you that I go away: for if I go not away, the Comforter will not come unto you; but if I depart, I will send him unto you" (KJV). What could be better than having Jesus here with us? Someone physical to take all our problems to. Yet the truth is that we are at an advantage with the Holy Spirit. He is God with us, in us, and upon us. The Holy Spirit is the one who produces love, joy, peace, patience, gentleness, kindness, goodness, faithfulness, and self-control in the life of the believer (Galatians 5:22).

A Case for Identity

Jesus said to the Samaritan woman at the well: "God is a Spirit, and they that worship him must worship in spirit and truth" (John 4:24 ASV). Paul wrote in 1 Corinthians 2:11: "For who among men knows the thoughts of a man except the man's spirit within him? In the same way no one knows the thoughts of God except the Spirit of God." Now we know we are made up of body, soul, and spirit; but the spirit is the authentic you, your heart. The one no one sees, except when the mouth reveals the heart. This helps us better understand the identity of the Holy Spirit, that he is not less or more in position or rank, But he is God—Hallelujah! if you want to know what God thinks of you, ask the Holy Spirit, he can tell you, he is the mind of God.

Peculiar Reward

The Spirit of God in you wants expression. The Holy Spirit in the life of a person works to teach, counsel, and comfort. He also brings insight, revelation, knowledge, and intimacy. When he is resting and abiding in you—aha!—then come the manifestations. When the Spirit of God rests on you, you become a sign and a wonder. Life's goodness, favor, and mercy become your fans. They follow you wherever you go because they see in you to whom they belong—the Holy Spirit. Throughout Scripture, there was no one whom the Holy Spirit was upon who did not do great things. Their lives were always significant in some way.

Not that our quest for a relationship with the Holy Spirit is for some professional gain, but it is a reward for knowing him. You never come before an earthly king and leave empty-handed, unless you were before a poor or counterfeit king. So, if an earthy king keeps such a code of honor, how much more so the King of Kings? With most kings, you can only come before their presence by invitation. Likewise the Father; his grace, through Jesus, is the invitation, but for intimacy, you must do the seeking. Taste and see— you have to come to the table that has already been prepared for you. Then and only then will you "see." He will not impose himself on anyone; you must go after this dimension. You must want it, become a yielded vessel, and subject your heart to his lordship.

Now this is eternal life: that they may know you, the only true God, and Jesus Christ, whom you have sent.—John 17:3

For the grandeur of the bride, there can be no room for ignorance. To access the treasures of heaven and our full inheritance in Christ, we need an encounter which brings transformation. "You shall know the truth, and the truth shall make you free" (John 8:32 NKJV). Without knowledge of the truth you cannot be free. At the cross, we were set free by the blood of Jesus, but it is the knowledge of the truth that makes us free. It's like a judge who ordered the release of a prisoner and gives the document of his release to the warden who somehow fails to deliver the documents to the prisoner. That prisoner has been set free, but has not been made free because he is unaware of his status. The greatest enemy of the believer is not the Devil but ignorance, and ignorance leads to frustration and unbelief.

The fact is, once we turn to Jesus, we are born into the kingdom of God and we become heirs of God. It is only wise that we get to know the One to whom we have returned. When we know him, we know our eternal identity, our position, and the inheritance we've been given. Jesus said, "This is eternal life: that they may know you, the only true God, and Jesus Christ, whom you have sent" (John 17:3). If eternal life is everlasting life, and God is everlasting, it then connotes that we have the God kind of life. And by experience, knowledge grants us access to an ongoing consciousness without intermission.

In the discovery of him, we also find who we are and to what purpose we were created. Discovering oneself does not happen in an instant. We grow in our discovery of self; so also we grow in our discovery of God. We can really know God through a relationship and not based solely on his acts. Therefore the children of Israel knew the acts of God, yet they kept sinning against him (Psalm 103:7), but when you KNOW Him, you cannot willfully sin against him.

When a relationship is based solely on what a person does or is doing, it lacks depth and therefore can easily be undone. Many know about God, have intellectual knowledge of him, but intimately knowing his ways requires depth. The ways of a person can only be known through proximity, relationship, and intimacy. Moses knew the ways of God because he had an intimate relationship with God, and he was counted a friend of God.

The LORD would speak to Moses face to face, as a man speaks with his friend. Then Moses would return to the camp, but his young aide Joshua son of Nun did not leave the tent. Moses said to the LORD, "You have been telling me, 'Lead these people,' but you have not let me know whom you will send with me. You have said, 'I know you by name and you have found favor with me.' If you are pleased with me, teach me your ways so I may know you and continue to find favor with you."—Exodus 33:11–13

Intimacy with the Lord is so critical that we can no longer walk unaware of our greatest opportunity: to know the creator of the universe face to face. If eternal life is in the knowledge of God, then we see why people perish for the lack of it (Hosea 4:6). To know God experientially is to behold his glory, to live from his presence, and that is the ultimate quest of humanity.

Whether we realize it or not, the human heart is in search of God, meaning, and significance. In the knowledge of him we find purpose and the answers to human existence—through the intimate knowledge of him we know his ways, and that only comes from spending time with him and communing with him.

To know his love, receive it, and love him in response. There is no treasure we desire that can be compared with finding Jesus; the One who created all things. He is the desire of the nations (Haggai 2:7). His price is far more than any choice gold because he owns it. Knowing him brings understanding—all things were created by him and for him, nothing was made without him. We were created to be with him, to be one with him, and to be like him, and in that lies all the answers to the questions of life. It is the single greatest achievement a person can attain on this human journey. We get to be friends with the creator of the universe. When we come to this knowledge of the creator, we become awakened co-creators. Once we encounter him, we are no longer permitted to stay the way we were, and all that he has becomes available to us.

"My people are destroyed for lack of knowledge" (Hosea 4:9 KJV). Not for lack of general knowledge or scientific knowledge, but lack of the knowledge of God. A knowledge that delivers insights and experience with the known, that helps you see from his perspective.

Christ died to restore your mind, to give you a mind that is at peace with God, and a mind with access to his unlimited knowledge. By knowing him we ultimately discover who we are and the purpose for which we were created. The only way to be fully persuaded of who we are and the authority we hold, is to live in a realm of oneness with the Father. This experience is available to every believer by the Holy Spirit—Go for it!

Process Brings Vulnerability

CHAPTER 13

For Love and Glory

The King is enthralled by your beauty; honor him, for he is your lord. - Psalms 45:11

We have extensively explored and know that all God does for and to us is for his love and glory. Jesus died because God so loved the us, the glory of God is revealed in the face of Jesus. And now, for these days he declares "I will glorify the house of My glory" (Isaiah 60:7). We must realize that God has made us to be amazing and captivating. In Christ, we are radiant and therefore we must live life from the point of majesty. Think of it! If you really believe God is glorious, and he lives in you, doesn't that make you Glorious?

As you grow in intimacy realize that you are the glory of God_ his masterpiece! Jesus came to give you heavens perspective which otherwise would not have been discovered. He came to teach us the language of heaven. A life so exuberant, over flowing with abundance, and filled with possibilities. Love and Glory is what eternal life offers, and we get to begin living in eternity the moment we are in Christ. Remember, eternal life is in knowing God (John 17:3), therefore our experience of him on earth will always mirror the quality of life eternity offers. That is, life as He knows it, not life as we know it. There is so much more to discover about the love and glory of God. Our journey is to discover the one who loves us with all of his heart. And this is an ongoing revelation by the Holy Spirit who leads us into all truth. We will continually grow in our knowledge of Him unto eternity.

All that God created he considered good, and that includes the justified you. Yes, we live in a world encumbered by evil and wickedness, but God is spellbound by the beauty he has bestowed upon you, a splendor accessible to all who will serve him with love and reverence, and for that we owe him the our lives.

We are rapidly entering the glory of the latter rain of God's outpouring. We are starting to see a shift in the messages of the church, the focus on Jesus is taking place, and a revival is on the way. For far too long we have focused

on many things, have been distracted by many things; we all know our distractions, but Jesus is returning for a radiant bride, one who is ready.

The Restoration Process of God's Glory

God gives us completion in Christ, then teaches us how to walk in it. King David sought after the restoration of God's glory to Israel after the reign of king Saul. But the restoration process had already began with the Prophet Samuel. Why is this important? Unlike the sudden manifestation of God's glory with Moses, God commissioned the prophet Samuel to prepare the people by calling them back to the heart of God. This is the sound of every true prophet: so Samuel said to all the Israelites, "if you are returning to the Lord with all your hearts, then rid yourselves of the foreign gods . . . and commit yourselves to the Lord and serve him only, and he will deliver you out of the hand of the Philistines." (1 Samuel 7:3)

We see that the coming glory is a process of returning to the heart of God. To experience a revival or any great move of God, there must be a returning. "If you return, then I will restore you—and you will stand;..."(Jeremiah 15:19 NASB). To stand before God is to be in his tangible presence.

"Blessed are the pure in heart for they will see God"(Matthew 5:8) **How do you see God?** Your heart sees him. A pure heart is a heart that loves God and true purity of heart is perfected both in the knowledge and fear of the Lord! Now anyone can say they love God, but the determining factor would be as Paul the Apostle makes it clear:

"Since, we have these promises, dear friends, let us purify ourselves from everything that contaminates body and spirit, perfecting holiness out of reverence for God." (2 Corinthians 7:1)

To see greater glory, the church/ bride must prepare her heart to receive the bridegroom. How do we prepare our hearts for the presence of the Lord? We must change the way we think. The kingdom of God is a different way of thinking, speaking, and acting; it's a different way of life.

• **Hunger:** (Luke 1:53) "He has filled the hungry with good things but has sent the rich away empty" The scripture above gives us an understanding of how God releases more to us. The hungry is the unsatisfied, and the dependent. The rich are those you are satisfied and have no need for more, they have arrived, and are comfortable. Hunger is designed to elevate you, it puts us in a place of expectation, humility, and dependency. Hunger is passion, a desire for progression, advancement, and increase. It has the ability to drive us from our place of comfort in quest for something or in this case, someone greater. To maintain fire and passion for God, hunger is a necessary requirement.

• **The Fear of the Lord:** (Proverbs 4:9) "The fear of the Lord is the beginning of wisdom"

The beginning place of the wisdom which comes from

God is **The Fear of the Lord,** and the fear of the Lord requires the knowledge of God. Wisdom is the act of thinking from heaven to earth. The knowledge of God brings us into revelation, and revelation invites us into intimacy. The point here is, The Fear of the Lord is a place of closeness, and absolute awe. It is the understanding of who God is and how close he wants to be. It is wise to read through the scriptures that speak of it; there is great treasure in imbibing it. We cannot come into intimacy or see greater glory without this fear. It is a fear of never parting from the presence of God.

• **Purified Heart:** (Proverbs 22:11) "He who loves purity of heart and has grace on his lips, will have the king for a friend."

Friendship with God is reserved only for the pure in heart. We must understand the characteristics of who God is_ He is King! Only a pure heart sees him for who he is, hence grace and approval is the fruit of the lips. What purifies the heart? The revelation of who God is, his goodness, and the greatness of his unfailing love. The result then, is a genuine love for Him. A heart that sees no fault in Him, keeps no offenses, has only good things to say of Him, and one who is merciful toward his fellow man.

• **Cooperation:** Ephesians 4:23-24

"To be made new in the attitude of your minds; and to

put on the new self, created to be like God in true righteousness and holiness."

Cooperating with God in the identity he has given you is extremely vital, if we are going to walk in the glory and be effective displays of his splendor, we must cooperate with the identity he has given us. The Holy Spirit is here to lead each of us into all truth, and one of the most profound truths is, there has been a divine exchange! We have been given a new life; the old man must be put off. You must believe what God says about you because heaven has record of your identity in Christ. Therefore, if you are not speaking the same language that heaven is speaking over you, you will be out of sync with your purpose and potentially undermine your destiny.

There are three primary ways in which to cooperate with God concerning your identity.

1). Align your mind with the mind of Christ, that is, how God thinks (From heaven to earth).

2). See from God perspective, the justified you (Truth).

3). Speak what He is speaking about you (Revelation).

When we think, speak, and see in alignment with God, our life and capacity increases, and progresses into a greater experience with God and the life he has given us.

The blessings and Promises of Intimacy

Key Scriptures

➤ Joy

"Those the LORD has rescued will return. They will enter Zion with singing; everlasting joy will crown their heads. Gladness and joy will overtake them, and sorrow and sighing will flee away." (Isaiah 51:11 NIV)

➤ Answers to prayer

"Before they call I will answer; while they are still speaking I will hear." (Isaiah 53:24) "If you remain in me and my words remain in you, ask whatever you wish, and it will be given you". (John 15:7)

➤ Protection

"How abundant are the good things that you have stored up for those who fear you, that you bestow in the sight of all, on those who take refuge in you. In the shelter of your presence you hide them from all human intrigues; you keep them safe in your dwelling from accusing tongues." (Psalm 31: 19-20)

> Revelation

"Who, then, is the man that fears the Lord? He will instruct him in the way chosen for him.... The Lord confides in those who fears him; he makes his covenant known to them". (Psalms 25:12,14)

> Provision

"Blessed are those you choose and bring near to live in your courts! We are filled with the good things of your house, of your holy temple". (Psalms 65:4)

> Peace

"yet my unfailing love for you will not be shaken nor my covenant of peace be removed". (Isaiah 54:10)

> Deliverance

"Because he hath set his love upon me, therefore I will deliver him: I will set him on high, because he hath know my name". (Psalms 91:14)

> Wealth "Bestowing wealth on those who love me and making their treasuries full".(Proverbs 8:21)

> Presence "If you are pleased with me, teach me your ways so I may know you and continue to find favor with you... The Lord replied, My presence will go with

you, and I will give you rest". (Exodus 33:13)

➢ **Sanctification** "Sanctify them by the truth; your word is truth... For them I sanctify myself, that they too may be truly sanctified". (John 17:17,19)

➢ **An Everlasting Covenant** I will make an everlasting covenant with you, my faithful love promised to David." (Isaiah 55:3)

➢ **Satisfaction** "Because your love is better than life... in your name I will lift up my hands. My soul will be satisfied as with the richest of foods...." (Psalms 63:3,4,5)

These are just a few promises from the many treasures in God's word. There are many more blessings to discover and uncover about what it means to be the beloved of the Most High God.

Epilogue

The Process of God is to bring you into the highest, purest, and truest revelation of your purpose and identity here on earth. It is to promote you in the spirit and carry you forward. It is to speed up your destiny and expose your rich inheritance. Where you rise up into a place of abundance and rich encounters with God.

It is no coincidence that you are in this season of your life; you must press in to discover who God wants to be for you. God is your master, but he is also your friend. He is your father, but he can also be your lover. He is the lily of the valley, but he is a consuming fire.

Where God wants to take you will require that you leave the remains of mediocrity behind. It requires a change of heart, and a renewing of your mind into a new place with God to scale new heights in life. Where you come into knowledge of the truth and discover who he is. Not as your church experience has depicted him, but in a personal experience with him as your testimony.

If you are willing to upgrade your experience, and take every limit off God, he will manifest to you the God of heaven and earth. **Built** into the encounter, is the unveiling of Gods perception about you; and in that lies the power to walk in the embrace of who he has called you to be (your identity).

There you can live in the majesty of his affection for you, courageous, undeterred, and indomitable.

A Prayer for Intimacy

Heavenly Father, thank you for loving me and choosing me before you formed the world. You are my Creator, my true Father, Redeemer, Helper, and the end of all things, including my life. I want to truly know you, and encounter your love. Thank you for proving your love to me when you sent your only Son, Jesus, to be the sacrifice for my new life. Draw me deeper into you as I seek to know you more. I love you; I worship you; I trust you. I give you total claim to my life, and from now on, I honor you as Lord over my life. Open my eyes to behold your majesty, and the beauty of who you truly are. I pray this in the name of Jesus Christ--- My Lord!

Now to Him who is able to keep you from stumbling and to present you faultless before the presence of His glory with exceeding joy, to God our Savior, who alone is wise, be glory and majesty, dominion and power, both now and forever. Amen!

–JUDE 24-25

ABOUT THE AUTHOR

IFY OKOH

Is a minister of the Good News. She is a passionate and gifted speaker who offers a refreshing perspective on the love of God and revelation knowledge. She has the zeal to inspire, empower, and give people a radiant idea of God. Her passionate, practical and often humorous presentation of Gods word touches the lives of those she comes in contact with. She resides in the state of Georgia with her husband, Joseph, and their four children.

It is her new nature to be Victorious, Steadfast, Anointed, and Thankful.

To learn more about her, go ahead and reach out, she promises to respond personally!

radiantlifeinternational@gmail.com

www.ifyokoh.com

Find her on **Instagram** @radiantlifeintl

ADDITIONAL RADIANT LIFE RESOURCES

Don't miss the teaching series based on the book. These materials are perfect for small group study, Sunday school service, or simply a deeper understanding and revelation of God's word. IFY's teaching style will engage even the most hesitant reader. The Process of God is available on E-Reader format and in Hard Copy.

The Process of God Video Seminar

For More information, please visit
www.ifyokoh.com

NOTES

"THE NEW AMERICAN STANDARD NEW TESTAMENT GREEK LEXICON IS BASED ON THAYER'S AND SMITH'S BIBLE DICTIONARY, PLUS OTHERS. IT IS KEYED TO THE LARGE KITTEL AND THE "THEOLOGICAL DICTIONARY OF THE NEW TESTAMENT."

[1] Nepios: νήπιος, 1 an infant, little child. 2 a minor, not of age. 3 metaphorically used for childish, untaught, unskilled.

[2] Paidion: "παιδίον, a young child." New American Standard Hebrew-Aramaic and Greek dictionaries, updated edition.

[3] Teknon: "τέκνον, descendant (Acts 2:39); disciple, one who follows a teacher in authority (3 John 4)." Dictionary of Biblical Languages with Semantic Domains: Greek.

[4] Huios: "υιός...those who revere God as their Father, the pious worshippers of God, those who in character and life resemble God, those who are governed by the Spirit of God, repose the same calm and joyful trust in God which children do in their parents (Romans 8:14, Galatians 3:26), and hereafter in the blessedness and glory of the life eternal will openly wear this dignity of the sons of God. Term used preeminently of Jesus Christ, as enjoying the supreme love of God, united to him in affectionate intimacy, privy to his saving councils, obedient to the Father's will in all his acts." Enhanced Strong's Lexicon.

[5] Teleios: "τέλειος... 1 brought to its end, finished. 2 wanting nothing necessary to completeness. 3 perfect. 4 that which is perfect. 4A consummate human integrity and virtue. 4B of men. 4B1 full grown, adult, of full age, mature." Enhanced Strong's

Lexicon.

Gnosis: knowledge signifies in general intelligence, understanding the general knowledge of Christian religion the deeper more perfect and enlarged knowledge of this religion, such as belongs to the more advanced esp. of things lawful and unlawful for Christians moral wisdom, such as is seen in right living.

Epignosis: precise and correct knowledge used in the NT of the knowledge of things ethical and divine acknowledge*1, knowledge 14, real knowledge 1, true knowledge 4

Ginosko: KNOW; KNOWLEDGE no, nol'-ej (in Hebrew chiefly yadha`, noun da`ath; in Greek ginosko, oida' "to know fully," epiginosko, noun gnosis
http://www.biblestudytools.com/encyclopedias/isbe/know-knowledge.html

Library - New American Standard, New Testament Greek Lexicon,

Chapter Two: Bruce Wilkinson (lecture, BreakThru to the next level conference, Kennesaw, Georgia, April 2014)

International Standard Bible Encyclopedia (Biblesoft, 1996) web.

Some sources are unknown.

---

www.ingramcontent.com/pod-product-compliance
Lightning Source LLC
Chambersburg PA
CBHW020544030426
42337CB00013B/970